£10.99

Heathers, Conifers and the Winter Garden

A Wisley Gardening Companion

Heathers, Conifers and the Winter Garden

FRANK KNIGHT, JOHN BOND, LYN RANDALL
and
ROBERT PEARSON

Cassell

The Royal Horticultural Society

THE ROYAL HORTICULTURAL SOCIETY

Cassell Educational Limited
Villiers House, 41/47 Strand
London WC2N 5JE
for the Royal Horticultural Society

This compilation copyright © Cassell/The Royal
Horticultural Society 1995

Heaths and Heathers copyright © Frank Knight 1972, 1986
Dwarf and Slow-Growing Conifers copyright © John Bond
and Lyn Randall 1987
The Winter Garden copyright © Robert Pearson 1989

First published 1995

British Library Cataloguing in Publication Data
A catalogue record for this book is available from the
British Library

ISBN 0–304–32073–0

Photographs by John Glover, Anne Hyde, Frank Knight,
Photos Horticultural, Lyn Randall, Peter Stiles,
W. H. D. Wince

Line drawings by Sue Wickison

Phototypesetting by RGM Associates, Southport

Printed in Hong Kong by Wing King Tong Co. Ltd.

Cover: Against a background tracery of bare branches, heathers, conifers and
other evergreens bring life and colour to the winter garden
    Photograph by Peter Stiles
Page 1: Winter jasmine and irises make a charming combination
    Photograph by Andrew Lawson
Page 2: This conifer garden is set in crazy paving for low maintenance
    Photograph by Photos Horticultural
Back cover: *Ilex aquifolium* 'J. C. van Thol'

Contents

The winter heaths create a carpet of colour, set off by bronze rhododendron foliage

Foreword

It gives me great pleasure to introduce another of the Society's Wisley Gardening Companions. In this volume, three more books in the popular and long-established Wisley Handbook series are brought together under one title: *Heaths and Heathers, Dwarf and Slow-growing Conifers* and *The Winter Garden*.

It always seems to me that heathers and conifers form one of the best of all plant partnerships. Their satisfying association owes much to the fact that most heathers tend to grow in one plane and are, therefore, much enlivened by the neat punctuations of dwarf conifers. If carefully planted neither overwhelms the other, and they share the virtue of being evergreen. In time they knit together to form a ground-covering blanket, impenetrable to weeds and remarkably undemanding to maintain. Although their singular forms and flowering potential give them year-round appeal, it is in the winter that their colour is most appreciated.

Whenever I walk round Wisley on a dank and dismal winter's day, the heather garden never fails to cheer me. Red- and yellow-stemmed dogwoods edging the Round Pond are coppiced to produce bright young shoots, and nearby are banks of crocuses. No! The garden in winter need never be dull.

It is in the winter that the structure and design of a garden becomes apparent. Small incidents can be appreciated: the modest flowers of witch hazel and *Viburnum farreri* smother bare branches and their delicate perfumes pervade the air; berries linger on the mountain ash and the branches of deciduous trees form a tracery against the sky. There is much to be admired in the winter garden, as this book will reveal.

Gordon Rae
Director General
The Royal Horticultural Society

The garden in winter need never be dull – with heathers, conifers and variegated evergreen shrubs

Heaths and Heathers

FRANK KNIGHT

Chamaecyparis pisifera 'Nana Aureovariegata' and
Erica × darleyensis 'J. W. Porter' provide rounded shapes on
different planes

Introduction

The common names, heaths and heathers, are used for three main genera – *Calluna, Daboecia* and *Erica*. There are few plants which have so deservedly gained recognition for their wide and effective use in modern gardening. The variations in size, habit of growth, colour of flower and foliage, and flowering times, together with the satisfactory way in which heathers blend with other plants in the garden, result in one of the most satisfying of garden features. As evergreens they contribute interest throughout the year. It is true that their use is restricted to suitable soil types, for with few exceptions heathers will not tolerate alkaline soils. Heaths and heathers are of particular use in cutting down work in the garden. When planted in groups each grows into its neighbour, so leaving little opportunity for weeds to grow.

A visit to any nursery or garden centre selling hardy trees and shrubs will show the wide range of heathers available. Today, many are grown in containers, so that planting can be carried out at almost any time of the year.

No garden is too large or too small for heathers to be fitted in, either as a complete heather garden, or in groups among shrubs, to cover sloping banks, or in the rock garden.

I strongly advise anyone who is planning to plant heathers to see as many existing heather gardens as possible. There are good examples at the Royal Horticultural Society's Garden at Wisley, the Savill Garden at Windsor, the Royal Botanic Gardens in Edinburgh and at Kew, the Liverpool University Botanic Garden, Ness, in Cheshire, and the Northern Horticultural Society's garden at Harlow Carr near Harrogate.

Although these are examples on a large scale, they clearly show effective planning and planting which can be adapted for any size of garden by adjusting the numbers of plants required and, if planning for a small garden, omitting those, such as the tree heaths, which will grow too large.

The heather garden at Wisley

Heathers in Nature

More species of *Erica* are to be found wild in southern Africa than in any other country, although these Cape heaths are not hardy here and so will not be considered further. The heathers which cover large tracts of moorland and mountain in Britain and the rest of Europe belong to the genera *Calluna*, *Daboecia* and *Erica*. These are the hardy heathers that we can grow outside.

Calluna vulgaris is the purple heather, or ling, of the mountains and moors, and the observant will notice a considerable variation in the habit of growth of the plants and also in colours of flowers and foliage. Plants may be small close-growing hummocks or shrubs up to 3 feet high (90cm).

Erica is the botanical name for heaths, but it is usual to include both *Calluna* and *Erica* in the term 'heather' – for instance the *heather* garden. The hardy species of *Erica* are natives of Europe, and eight are found in the British Isles. All are evergreen shrubs, with very small linear leaves. The flowers are produced in abundance at the ends of the shoots, and do not drop when they fade, remaining on the stems and turning to an attractive russet brown colour.

Daboecia, the third member of the heaths and heathers, includes two species but only one is usually seen in gardens. *Daboecia cantabrica*, St Dabeoc's heath, is a native of Ireland, where it is often found threading itself through the autumn-flowering gorse.

The conditions in which these plants grow in Europe are broadly similar. The ericas and *Calluna* cover large areas of higher land where the soil is usually rather poor and the rainfall sometimes high. Some grow in damp places, others where the soil dries out in summer. These are usually exposed parts of the country with little protection from cold and strong winds.

It is worth mentioning some of the individual needs among ericas. For instance, *Erica ciliaris*, Dorset heath, although growing in moist soils in nature (not swamps), will tolerate drier conditions in cultivation. *Erica cinerea* always grows in drier places than *Calluna*. *Erica tetralix*, cross-leaved heath, grows wild in wetter conditions than most other species and thrives in wet bogs where cotton grass may be a companion plant. Although native of Cornwall and Ireland, *Erica vagans* (Cornish heath) grows well in cultivation as far north as the Moray Firth;

'Gold Tips', a cultivar of *Erica* x *veitchii*

it will tolerate slightly alkaline soil conditions. *Erica carnea* and its numerous cultivars will also tolerate alkaline soils. At Wisley this heather grew successfully on a steep, north-facing bank. Two taller heathers are *Erica arborea* (tree heath) and *E. lusitanica* (Portuguese heath); both are liable to be damaged in severe winters, but both are tolerant of slightly alkaline soil conditions.

The environment in which heathers grow wild tends to be harsh, with poor soil and little shelter. They are brought up to a tough life, but given a little care in the garden will repay the gardener for many seasons. The only condition is that heathers must be planted in full sun.

Heathers in the Garden

The question of planting to reduce maintenance crops up many times in the life of a professional nurseryman. Heather gardening contributes largely to saving labour and particularly by cutting down weeding.

The use of heathers in the garden can vary from planting small groups along the foot of shrub borders or beds, the formation of a formal edging along the side of a path (but this does not appeal to me), in beds consisting entirely of heathers with a few carefully selected and sited dwarf or slow-growing conifers and other suitable shrubs (for suggestions see pp. 67–73), in the rock garden, and best of all, where there is room, in a separate heather garden. In short there is every reason, given suitable soil conditions, for all gardens to have their quota of heathers, for these will provide colour throughout the year.

CHOICE OF SITE

From my experience of gardening in several parts of the United Kingdom, on soils varying in texture and with annual rainfall amounts from 20 to 45 inches (500–1200 mm), I can say that heathers will thrive in a wide range of conditions. They like to be in the sunshine since if planted in shade they become straggly and soft in growth and fail to flower freely. It will have been noticed, however, that an exception cited earlier was *Erica carnea*, growing on a northern slope at Wisley; I want to emphasise that there is a difference between growing in an open exposed northern slope and under the shade of trees, and the latter is not a suitable situation for heathers.

Many sloping grass banks which are difficult to maintain can be planted with heathers and rocks installed to provide an additional attractive feature. Such an arrangement associated with the right shrubs could transform an area that was a troublesome chore into one of low maintenance.

PREPARATION OF THE SOIL

Preparation for planting heathers normally consists of single digging, breaking up the soil and removing all weeds. Perennial weeds, in particular all pieces of bindweed and couch grass, must

A mixture of *Erica carnea* in Windsor Great Park

be removed; they are very difficult to control after planting. Single digging means digging to a depth of one spade. Peat should be worked into the soil (but be sure the peat is damp); I prefer to do this by spreading a layer up to 2 inches deep (5 cm) over the surface of the ground after digging and working this in around the roots when planting, taking care to mix it in with the soil.

In a heavy clayey soil drainage can be improved by throwing up the soil when digging so that the level of the bed is a few inches above that of the surrounding soil. This raised area will dry out more quickly as the water drains down to the lower level. Adding a generous supply of organic material will also help to improve a heavy soil.

On lighter and stony soils heathers will grow satisfactorily, and there is no need to make the raised beds as the drainage on these types of soils is likely to be very good. In a hot dry period the drainage will probably be too sharp, but the water-holding capacity of the soil can be improved by mixing in capacity of the soil can be improved by mixing in organic material, and mulching with pulverised bark.

The important point to be emphasised is that thorough preparation of the soil before planting will result in vigorous, healthy growth of the plants.

DESIGN AND LAYOUT

The design of a heather garden is a matter of scale and balance, demanding the adaptation of the available site, summing up its setting and size, and then designing and carrying out a planting scheme which fits. In the large heather garden at the west end of Seven Acres in Wisley Garden fewer than about fifty plants of one kind would be inadequate. In an average sized garden groups of twenty-five, fifteen or even fewer plants would look right.

The ideal, of course, is to be able to plant the whole heather garden in one co-ordinated operation. Where this is possible I like to have the area prepared in the manner I have described and then, to invest the scheme with character, the soil on a flat or even surface can be skilfully undulated so that the planting looks natural. This can be done by building up gently rounded mounds of soil, not sharp peaks, between which will be valleys, and these mounds and valleys will be accentuated by planting drifts of taller growing plants on the mounds and lower spreading kinds in the valleys. There is so much one can accomplish on a flat site by adopting some of the effects to be seen in the wild.

Heathers in Adrian Bloom's garden at Bressingham, Norfolk, provide year-round interest

Having prepared the site and given it some character the next operation is to plan the planting. This can be done in two main ways, the first being that of taking a fairly accurate survey of the site to be planted and plotting this on a drawing board to a workable scale, for example that of an inch (2.5 cm) to 8 feet (2.4 m). Assuming that the choice of heathers has already been made, the next question is how many of each are required and how to arrange them. For this, information is needed on the colours of the flowers and foliage, times of flowering and particularly the eventual size of the plants. In addition allowance must be made for including other plants, such as *Gaultheria mucronata* and conifers, which associate well with heathers.

The sizes of the individual groups will depend mainly on the size of the site. This also influences the provision of suitable paths. On a large scale grass paths may be appropriate; in small schemes paths through the heathers may not be needed and flat stepping-stones or just the beaten earth will suffice. There is always the danger of being 'too tidy' and I do not like to see a neatly edged lawn meeting the natural growth of the plants; I like to see irregular paths following the natural run of the ground.

It is now that scale and balance take over. In designing the irregular shapes of the planting areas which each group will occupy, I have derived much help by thinking of a coloured map of England where the counties in their different shapes and sizes are portrayed by different colours. These make ideal pictures in the mind of groups of heathers which can be adapted and transferred to a drawing. Next comes the work of filling in the names and quantities of the plants to be used.

In all planting schemes worked out on a drawing board I find it practical to make a careful list of the plants I wish to use. I divide my list under the three main headings, tall, intermediate and low growing kinds, and then fill in details on dimensions, colour of flower and foliage, and time of flowering. I call this my master list and treat it as if it were a reservoir of plant material into which I dip as the planning progresses, transferring the names of the particular plants to the positions I decide as appropriate on the plan. Small points, such as doing the original work on the drawing with a soft pencil, should be kept in mind, for seldom will the first scheme be the last one.

Spacing of the individual plants to be used within each localised group is of primary importance. I know that there is some disagreement, and in the following I give my basic distances and leave it to others either to adopt or adapt them. I like to establish a complete cover over the ground as quickly as possible, and therefore space the smaller growing cultivars of *Erica carnea*, such

as 'King George', at one foot apart (30 cm). The larger growing cultivars of *E. carnea*, such as 'Springwood White' need more room, 15 inches or more (37 cm) (see list on pp. 49 for measurements). *Calluna vulgaris* and its tall cultivars such as 'Alportii' I space at 15 inches (37 cm), *Erica erigena (mediterranea)* at 2 feet 6 inches (75 cm) and tree heathers at 4 feet (1.2 m). Some people may think that my spacing of the smaller growing kinds is too close, but these are the distances I have found practical after planting thousands of heathers. Within the pattern I have set out there are many heathers and heaths of intermediate growth and spacing can therefore be adjusted. For myself, if ever I find I am caught hesitating between spreading out or closing up the spacing I close up. The sooner the ground is covered and the weeds excluded the better. With planting at wider distances than those I have given above, the plant canopy over the soil takes longer to meet and to suppress the weeds. Plants that are relatively widely spaced do, however, become a better, individual shape, because they are not competing with their neighbours; but this is not my way of growing heathers.

The most practical method for transferring a paper plan to the soil is to mark out the planting scheme on the ground. With this method the pencil used for drawing gives place to canes and labels. We are back at the stage where the ground has been dug and gentle mounds and little valleys have been made. The soil surface will need to be reasonably fine so that marking out is not made too difficult through encountering too many obstructions. The same mind picture of the final scheme must dominate as when designing on the drawing board, so cull information from the reservoir of plant material to be used and the shapes of the English counties on the map.

Sum up the whole site so that the irregularly shaped groups can be marked out on the ground in an appropriate and balanced way. Then take a stick or tool handle and mark out the boundaries of the various groups on the surface of the soil by a depression sufficiently deep to be readily seen; this can easily be filled in if the first shapes are not right. As a precaution, and particularly if there is a chance of the marks being obliterated by rain before planting, then some sand or sawdust can be strewn along the channels to show where they are.

I find that I make a better job if the marking out of the planting scheme is completed in one operation, simply because I may not always be in the mood to pick up where I left off.

Above: 'King George', a small growing cultivar of *Erica carnea*. Below: The larger 'Springwood White' (see pp. 51 and 52)

Spacing when planting heathers (see pp. 19–21)

Having finally decided that the scheme marked out is a good one, the next step is to fill in the groups. Whereas on the drawing board the names of the plants to be used will be written in the appropriate spaces on the planting plan, in the open-ground scheme labels are placed on the individual marked out groups, either labels which are stuck in the ground or paper labels tied to canes. In both cases a control list with the names of the plants to be used must be prepared beforehand and the names and quantities written on the labels. Knowledge of the plants to be used and imagination to visualise the end result are both essential in placing the right labels in the right positions. Based on my own experience it will, I think, be found that one acquires a flair for what is required, a rather slow hesitant uncertainty at the beginning seems suddenly to give way to a creative urge to get on and 'make a good job of it'. One begins to enjoy the exercise and when the final adjustment of the labels has been made there comes a feeling of deep satisfaction. Here I repeat the advice given earlier to visit and study existing established heather gardens, and adapt what is seen, to ensure that the planting is pleasing to one's self.

The heather garden at the Northern Horticultural Society's Garden, Harlow Carr, Yorkshire

Planting

WHEN TO PLANT

Now that container-grown plants are widely available, the time when it is possible to plant many shrubs, including heaths and heathers, has been greatly extended. Great emphasis used to be placed on planting heathers in the autumn and the spring, but in those days the plants were largely raised in the open ground. While the best times to plant are still between early October and early December, and late February to mid-April, it is now possible to plant in winter provided that the soil is not frozen, and in summer provided that the plants are kept well watered. Another advantage of buying container-grown plants (and in addition to garden centres, most specialist suppliers of heathers will also be able to provide plants in pots) is that there is less urgency to plant immediately, and the work can be conveniently spread over as long a period as one wishes.

HOW TO PLANT

After the preparation of the soil has been carried out, and the plants obtained, the actual planting is carried out. The planting distances given on p. 21 need not be adhered to rigidly, but it is generally more satisfactory if the plants do not overlap from one group to the next.

Having made sure that the complete balls of soil in which the plants have been growing are thoroughly saturated, remove them from their containers. It will usually be found that the plants are so well established in their containers that there is a 'cocoon' of roots enclosing the balls of soil. This should be loosened and separated out by prodding with the tines of a hand fork, or a strong sharply pointed stick. Never plant with the roots in a close matted state, as this results in the plants just sitting in the ground for too long a time before new roots are pushed out into the surrounding soil.

Another problem is what to do with the roots which have grown through the drainage holes of clay or plastic pots. There may sometimes be more roots outside than inside the pots, particularly when they have been standing on a bed of peat or similar material. The temptation is to wrench off the protruding roots, but this

Above, removing the plant from its polythene bag and, below, firming in the plant

upsets the balance between top growth and the root system, so that the tip shoots start to die back. Plants in plastic pots, which usually have several drainage holes, are sometimes difficult to deal with, and I usually cut these downwards from the rim with an old pair of secateurs to release the root system. Plants grown in polythene film containers are easily removed. I always remove any drainage crocks which may have been placed in the bottoms of the pots, but the old practice of crocking when growing heathers is not so often met with now.

The heathers having been set out they now have to be planted. A trowel is the best tool for this. It is more practical to start planting at the point farthest away from a path or lawn and work towards the point of completion. A skilled gardener works with rhythm, making up the surface of the ground as he proceeds, leaving the minimum of tidying up to be done at the finish.

The depth of planting should be such that the point where the base of the stems of the heathers emerges from the soil in the container is buried about an inch (2.5 cm) below the surface of the ground. This allows for settling and the top of the ball of soil will finally come just below the surface. Planting should be firm and the peat on the surface worked in around the roots of the plants. Avoid planting too deeply as this results in new fine roots being developed on the buried portion of the stems with a corresponding lack of new root action from the old root system; in times of drought the delicate roots on the stems will suffer.

So much for container-grown plants, but what of those which have been dug up from the open ground? With these the objective is to prevent the exposed roots from drying out between the time of lifting and replanting. Too many plants should not be laid out at one time. It is better to leave most where they keep moist and only unpack convenient quantities as they can be planted. It is obvious that one does not have the same freedom of handling as with container-grown plants, for each time a plant has to be moved it will mean that some of the fine soil adhering to its roots must be shaken off. Although more care has to be taken when planting open-ground plants they have one advantage over the container-grown specimens in that their root systems do not need to be dealt with so drastically.

So far I have been describing the work required in planting a new heather garden, but there are no fundamental differences in dealing with more modest schemes. If only part of a shrub border or some heather beds are involved, the advice already given can be adapted. The ground preparation will be the same and there will be no difference in handling the plants. Appropriate schemes can be attained by planting small groups of different kinds to give a more striking display over a shorter time. The same applies to planting heathers in a rock garden or on a sloping bank.

A mature planting of heathers shows just how well these shrubby plants 'knit' together in time

A corner of a heather garden

Aftercare

Heathers will need some attention after planting and it will be found that this settles down in normal conditions to a repetitive programme. After autumn and winter planting the plants will need to be firmed following a period of frost, and the staking and tying of the tree heaths should be checked. Snow lodging in the taller growing plants can be carefully shaken off to prevent or reduce branches breaking under its weight. Spring and summer planting may be followed by a drought and a good soaking should be given when needed; it is best to apply the water in the evenings, so that the plants can absorb the moisture in the lower temperatures overnight.

Weeding will be required during the first year or two but will get less as the plants grow together. If the ground has been thoroughly cleaned beforehand, the only problems will be with annual weeds. Maintaining a good mulch with pulverised tree bark will help suppress germination of weed seeds already in the soil. Any windborne or bird-dropped seeds germinating in the loose mulch can be killed by light hoeing on a dry sunny day. If perennial weeds do appear, try carefully extracting with a hand fork when the soil is moist. If, after heathers have been established for at least two years, perennial weeds appear, some kinds may be checked by applying the soil-acting herbicide dichlobenil in early spring before new growth begins, in strict accordance with manufacturers' instructions. No other herbicide is approved for garden use amongst heathers.

PRUNING

Some moderate cutting back does give good results in shaping the plants and maintaining their vigour.

For pruning, heaths and heathers can be divided into three groups: 1. summer flowering; 2. winter flowering; 3. tree heaths, such as *Erica australis*, *E. erigena (mediterranea)* and *E. terminalis*.

The summer flowering kinds should be very lightly pruned in the first half of March every year by cutting back, with a pair of sharp garden shears, the old flower heads to a point just below the bottom flowers on the stems. Do not cut back in the old wood. This pruning is followed by the production of vigorous shoots which will provide flowers of a high quality in the summer. If

A heather garden in winter

plants are left unpruned the new growths tend to be stubby and the flower spikes shorter.

The winter flowering kinds are cut back in the same way immediately after flowering to a point below the bottom flowers. This is normally done in late March and early April.

It will be found in practice that with heathers and heaths which tend to be procumbent in growth more skill is required in getting at the points where pruning should be done. But the care spent on the plants will be amply repaid, by better growth and flowering.

The third group does not need annual pruning. If the plants need to be rejuvenated, or reduced in size, cutting back can be done in late April or early May. It is difficult to prescribe a general operation, and generally it is best to take each plant or group of plants on its merits. Straggling branches can be shortened with secateurs, and the tall leading branches of *Erica arborea* which are outstripping all the others and making the bushes look 'thin' can be cut back to restore more balanced growth. If rejuvenation

Erica cinerea 'Eden Valley', which flowers from early June (see p. 59)

is needed, but the bushes are fairly healthy (i.e. their leaves are green) then fairly drastic cutting back can be carried out. Even if severely damaged by frost and snow most plants will respond well to hard pruning. New shoots are usually produced and by the second season most of them will be growing vigorously again.

In the wild, heather is often burnt every few years to provide new young shoots for the sheep, but this method of promoting fresh growth is not for the garden.

MULCHING

I like to give my plants an annual mulch with pulverised bark in spring after the pruning has been done, worked in between the plants to form a surface layer about half an inch deep (1.5 cm). Well rotted garden compost is an alternative mulching material.

Propagation

Nearly all the heaths and heathers which we grow in our garden are cultivars and must therefore be propagated vegetatively because they do not come true from seed. Two types of vegetative propagation that are commonly used to propagate heathers are described below.

LAYERING

For the amateur who wishes to raise small stocks of heathers in his garden and has no specialised equipment for propagation by cuttings, layering is the method which requires a minimum of skill or equipment. Layering means treating the stems of the plant before removing it from the plant so that new roots are produced; the rooted portions are then removed and planted to form new plants.

There are various ways of doing this. If the parent plant is to be retained without spoiling or moving it, a few branches around the perimeter can be selected and pegged to the ground so that a few inches of the stems are buried. It is usual to loosen the surface of the soil and mix in a little sand and peat or a peat alternative to form a small propagation bed. The selected stems are firmly fixed into this, using wooden pegs or bent wires, or even by placing stones on the branches. I find the use of stones clumsy and prefer pegs. It is not necessary to cut or scrape the stems before burying them. Layering is very successful if done in late September and October. After about a year, sufficient roots are established to enable the new plants to be cut from the parent plant and then preferably planted in a nursery-bed for about six months before putting them in their permanent positions.

Another simple method of layering is to part the branches of the growing plant at the soil surface and sprinkle in between a mixture of sand and peat or peat alternative. Press this down as firmly as possible so that the branches root into it. Topping up can be done as the material gets washed in by the winter rains. This method of layering can also be done in the autumn.

Above: Layering by (left) making a trench round the plant, then (right) spreading out the branches and filling in the centre
Below: *Erica tetralix* 'Pink Star' flowers from June to October (see p. 60)

The object in both the methods described should be to get vigorous young plants and not to try to root long straggling branches. In the second method the mound should rise so that the rooting takes place as near as possible to the active green leafy portions, in order to provide shapely plants. Sometimes in order to get larger plants more quickly several of the newly rooted young stems are bunched together and planted as one unit.

CUTTINGS

More heathers are raised from cuttings than by any other method and today there are several successful ways in which this can be done. One is to insert them in pots or pans and place these in a warm frame or greenhouse. The current method used at Wisley is as follows:

Cuttings, 2½ inches long (6 cm), are taken in July, either of tip growths or side growths pulled off from the branches with a heel, that is with a very small portion of the branch adhering to the base of the cutting. If the heel should be long and ragged it is trimmed off with a sharp knife or razor blade; no leaves are removed from the cuttings. They are inserted about ½ inch (1.5 cm) deep in a mixture of 2 parts sand and 1 part sphagnum moss peat in 5- or 6-inch diameter pans (15 cm), in which a piece of broken pot has been placed to prevent the mixture filtering through the drainage hole. Normally a 5-inch pan will take 50 to 60 cuttings. The pans are placed on a bed of sand on an open staging with a bottom heat of 70°F (21°C) in a warm greenhouse under an intermittent mist spray controlled by an electronic leaf or balance switch.

The cuttings produce sufficient roots in three to six weeks, depending on the species or cultivar, and are then potted singly into 2½-inch pots (6 cm), or pricked off at the rate of 30 rooted cuttings into 2½-inch deep seed trays (6 cm). The compost used is two parts acid loam, two parts moss peat and one part sand.

The trays or pots are then put into cold frames, which are kept closed at first. Then as the new young plants become established, air is admitted until finally the frame lights are removed, at first for limited periods in suitable weather but replaced during bad weather in the winter. In the first spring after the initial insertion of the cuttings, the young plants are ready for planting out in the open straight into their permanent position or into a nursery bed until the following autumn.

The amateur gardener without mist or a cold frame can still easily propagate from cuttings. The cuttings are taken in July, but the shoots selected are shorter than those for rooting under mist, and are about 1 to 1¼ inches long (2.5–3 cm). The cuttings are not

Juniperus scopulorum 'Skyrocket' provides a striking contrast to heathers

A generous planting of Erica × *darleyensis* 'Margaret Porter' is backed by the unusual mahonia M. *piperiana*

trimmed and are inserted in the same mixture as above, either in pots which are then put in a closed cold frame, or direct in the cold frame. The former is preferred because then each cultivar can be kept separate; they can then be hardened off as they become rooted. This is important because there is a variation in the speed of rooting between many heather species and cultivars.

If you do not have a cold frame the pots can be put outside in the garden in a shady place, e.g. at the foot of a north-facing wall. The microclimate around the cuttings can be kept uniform in temperature and humidity by enclosing the pots in closed plastic bags, or preferably by using clear plastic domes. These are more satisfactory than plastic bags because they do not sag over the cuttings.

When I was at Kew we used bell-glasses and there is no doubt their use is comparatively trouble-free. It is not easy to obtain bell-glasses today although plastic 'bell-jars' are available. There are also ready-made propagators consisting of a plastic tray with a clear plastic cover in which is some means of ventilation. With one of these the amateur can root heather cuttings without the help of special propagating frames or other equipment. The bell-glass should be sited in the open garden in a position not exposed to the sun otherwise the temperature will fluctuate too widely between day and night. The small area of propagating bed required can be clearly defined by pressing the rim of the bell-glass (or other container) firmly on the surface of the soil. Within this shape excavate the soil with a hand fork to a depth of 3 inches (7.5 cm) and replace it with a mixture of 3 parts of fine peat or peat alternative and 1 part of sharp lime-free sand. Make this firm so that the finished surface is about half an inch (1.5 cm) above the soil surrounding the bell-glass. Water well, with a fine rose, about twenty-four hours before inserting the cuttings.

I prefer to take cuttings in early October. Short flowerless side-shoots of the current year's growth are taken from the parent branches about an inch long (2.5 cm). Although not strictly necessary, I still like to pull away the tiny shoots from the side of the older branches, and with a very sharp knife or razor-blade trim the minute heel at the base of the cutting. There is no need to remove the leaves. The cuttings are then inserted in the bed of peat or peat alternative and sand to about half of their length by using a fine dibber to make the individual holes. The cuttings must be firmly inserted, spaced about half an inch apart (1.5 cm). The cuttings should be watered-in and I like to finish off by sprinkling some very dry silver sand to fill in the irregularities on the surface. This is like sifting sugar on a cake. The circular area having been satisfactorily filled, the bell-glass is placed firmly over the cuttings, taking care that there is no space between the rim of the glass and the soil.

If the cuttings have been taken in October no attention is needed during the winter, except to keep a watchful eye on the fine soil surface in case this may be disrupted by worm casts; I have even had my work upset by a mole. The debris from worm casts should be removed and the surface firmed.

A little more attention will be needed from early March onwards. It is not unusual at that time to get warm days and this is when rooting will be accelerated. If there is a tendency for the soil around the bell-glass to dry out, water round without removing it. As the spring develops, and according to the weather, a little air can be admitted gradually by placing a wedge under the rim of the glass. To begin with this can be done for no more than two or three hours in the middle of the day, but the period of ventilation can be gradually increased until the whole glass can be removed for a time. By the end of June it can be left off altogether. It is impossible to set down a precise calendar of operations, so much depends on the weather.

In August or September the tiny rooted cuttings can be carefully pricked off into boxes or planted in a specially prepared nursery bed. The young plants are left there for about one year to grow on into a suitable size for transplanting to their permanent site.

SEEDS

Some plants can be raised from seeds and one often sees self-sown seedlings growing near the parent plants. For example, Erica terminalis has regenerated naturally in the chalky soil in the garden at Highdown, near Worthing in Sussex. I also remember establishing broad paths of Calluna vulgaris in a large woodland-moorland garden bordering Chobham Common. This was done by gathering branches of the Calluna from the wild when the seeds were ripe and shaking these over the path areas so that the seeds were scattered on the prepared surface of the ground. The result was very good. In another garden at Windlesham Moor heather paths which were established by this method were kept short and springy by regularly cutting the plants with an old lawnmower.

Above: Calluna vulgaris 'Annemarie', with double flowers produced in summer (see p. 52)
Below: The crimson flowers of Calluna vulgaris 'Darkness' (see p. 53) constrasting with the bright green foliage of Erica lusitanica 'George Hunt' (see p. 52)

Problems

PESTS

Heaths and heathers in gardens are little affected by pests. Rabbits are sometimes a nuisance when they graze down young plants and they are, of course, likely to be abundant on light sandy soils. Various proprietary chemical repellants are partially effective in preventing damage but such protection as they afford is likely to break down in the winter when alternative food supplies are limited. In these circumstances only physical barriers, such as small-mesh wire netting, will give young plants complete protection. Once plants are established they can usually tolerate a certain amount of grazing without permanent harmful effect.

Other pests, such as the heather beetle and the heather gall midge are only of minor importance in gardens, although the heather beetle may do temporary damage to ling growing wild on moorlands.

DISEASES

Very few diseases of heathers have been recorded in Britain. Those occurring most frequently are as follows:

Erica wilt or browning (*Phytophthora cinnamomi*). This disease has, in recent years, become very troublesome on certain cultivars of *Calluna vulgaris*, *Erica carnea*, *E. cinerea*, *E. erigena* (*mediterranea*), *E. vagans* and *Erica* × *darleyensis*. The first obvious symptom is a silvering of the leaves on one or two shoots, the tips of which wilt. Within a few weeks some or all of the shoots die back, the affected plant loses many of its leaves and those which remain turn brown: occasionally, however, all the leaves become either grey or brown but are retained by the plant.

The fungus which causes this disease can attack a wide range of plants including conifers and rhododendrons. It is soil-borne and is encouraged by wet soil conditions. Infection occurs through the roots and most takes place during the summer when the soil is warm. The fungus produces thick-walled resting spores which can probably survive in the soil for several years and these can only be killed by steam sterilisation of the soil or by the use of soil sterilants which are not available to amateur gardeners. The disease is, therefore, difficult to control in small gardens and the best method is to dig up and burn or dispose of plants suspected of having the disease. Heathers should not be replanted where this disease has occurred unless the soil is first changed.

Unfortunately this disease can be positively identified only by specialised laboratory techniques and even then the results are not necessarily conclusive. Similar symptoms can, of course, be induced by adverse soil conditions and cultivated heathers can be affected in soils that are too dry, as well as too wet, even though they grow naturally in light soils which are inclined to dry out quickly. Should there be any doubt as to whether the discoloration of heather plants is due to faulty root action or erica wilt, it is recommended that, after removal of dead and dying shoots, the plants be sprayed fairly frequently during the growing season with a foliar feed. Nutrients applied in this form are taken in fairly rapidly by the leaves and the plants should receive a quick boost in vigour which will, in turn, encourage the development of new roots to replace those which have been injured or killed by the adverse soil conditions. If the plants do not recover after this treatment, they should be burned and the soil changed.

Honey fungus (*Armillaria* species). This fungus, is the most dangerous of all soil-borne parasites and can attack almost any type of plant. It has been known to kill plants of *Andromeda*, *Calluna* and *Erica*. The fungus kills the plant outright, and can be seen as fan-shaped masses of white fungal growth beneath the bark around the collar of the dead plant. Sometimes the brownish root-like structures (rhizomorphs), by which the fungus spreads through the soil, can be seen attached to the larger dead roots.

Affected plants should be dug up and burnt and the soil be changed completely. If possible, the source of infection (which may be an old stump or dead plant in a privet hedge for instance) should be traced and removed. If the trouble persists expert advice should be sought.

Rhizomorph fungus (*Marasmius androsaceus*). This fungus may kill plants of *Calluna* in Scotland, particularly in wet areas. It produces brown toadstools which soon turn black; these are very small, being about $1\frac{1}{4}$ inches high (3cm) with a cap of $\frac{1}{4}$ inch (5mm) and are not, therefore, easily seen. The toadstools are formed from July to November and produce numerous spores which give rise to more fungus plants, each of which produces fine black thread-like structures (rhizomorphs) which can be found at any time of the year wound round the heather stems. The rhizomorphs enter the stems and kill them so that the whole plant dies out. Affected plants should be removed and burned or disposed of as there is no way of controlling the disease.

Choosing Heathers

The choice of heather material is bewildering at first. Although there are relatively few species, there are hundreds of cultivars varying in flower colour, time of flowering and leaf colour. I will give first some details of the species and hybrids followed by a selection from the cultivars.

SPECIES

Calluna

Calluna vulgaris (heather, ling) grows up to 3 feet (90 cm), making a straggly, evergreen bush. The flowers are usually purplish pink but there are many variations in colour. The main flowering period is from July to November.

Daboecia

The species usually found in British gardens is *D. cantabrica*, a native of western Europe. It grows to 2 feet (60 cm), and the broad leaves are dark green above and whitish below. The flowers are rosy purple, oval, on the ends of the shoots, June to October. October.

Erica

The range of variation in ericas is very wide, and covers not only flower and leaf colour, but height, and among the species listed below tree heaths are included as well as the low growing kinds.

Erica arborea, tree heath, grows wild in a wide area around the Mediterranean, even down to the equator in Africa. It is not usually fully hardy here. It will grow up to to 20 feet (6 m), but is usually less than half this in cultivation in Britain. The leaves are bright green. Flowers are produced from February to April, and are nearly pure white, although sometimes with a pinkish tinge. Plants are always supplied in pots as they do not transplant well from the open ground. They need to be staked and tied after planting. The bushy habit should be encouraged by cutting back

Above: The tall Spanish heath *Erica australis* bears abundant bloom in midsummer (see p. 44)
Below: The Mediterranean *Erica erigena*, a small to medium shrub (see p. 44)

leading shoots that are too vigorous. It will tolerate mildly alkaline soils.

Erica australis, the Spanish heath, grows to about 4 feet (1.2m). It tends to spread out and does not always regain its original form after snow has lodged in the branches. The fragrant, bright purplish red flowers are produced in profusion in May and June, making an important link in the continuity of flowering. One of the most effective groupings of it that I have seen is with the Warminster broom (*Cytisus* × *praecox*). There is also a white flowered cultivar, 'Mr Robert', that was collected in southern Spain.

Erica ciliaris, the Dorset heath, is a native of south-west Europe, and of Dorset, Cornwall and west Ireland. It forms a low-growing shrub, up to 12 inches high (30 cm), with ascending shoots. The flowers are usually bright pink, and larger than most other ericas, being produced from July to October.

Erica cinerea, bell heather, is widely distributed in western Europe including the British Isles, forming a stiff branching shrub up to 24 inches tall (60 cm). When propagating I have noticed that as it grows on from rooted cutting to maturity it does not produce such a mass of very fine roots as do other species; plants tend to become surface rooting with fewer, larger main roots. The flowers are typically rosy purple, borne from June to September. It is particularly effective when seen with the dwarf gorses, *Ulex minor* or *U. galli*.

Erica erigena (*E. mediterranea*) comes from south western France, Spain and Portugal, and also western Ireland. It forms a vigorous, upright shrub of 3 to 12 feet tall (90 cm–3.6 m), producing purplish pink flowers from March to May. It is lime-tolerant and useful to provide height particularly in small gardens where *E. arborea* is too tall. The wood is brittle and branches are liable to snap if weighed down by snow, so knock it off as early as possible.

Erica carnea, one of the best known of the heaths, is native of the mountains of central and southern Europe. It tolerates alkaline soil and is very hardy. Plants grow up to 6 inches tall (15 cm), being spreading in habit. The flowers are usually rosy red although there is a wide range of colour among the cultivars. It flowers during the period October to April, so no other heather contributes so much cheerfulness to the winter garden.

Erica lusitanica (Portuguese heath) is native of south west Europe and naturalised in south west England. It is a lovely plant even when not in flower, growing up to 8 feet (2.4 m) with feathery branches of pale green leaves. The tubular flowers are pinkish in bud opening to white; the main flowering period is March to May. Although not reliably hardy, *E. lusitanica* will tolerate mildly alkaline soils.

Erica mackayana is a native of Co. Galway and Donegal, and also north-west Spain. An attractive plant, it grows to 9 in. (22 cm) high and bears rose coloured flowers between July and September.

Erica scoparia ssp. *scoparia*, besom heath, is rarely grown in gardens; dwarf 'Minima' ('Pumila') is more often seen. Its value is in providing contrast between its dark glossy green leaves and dense habit of growth, and the coloured-leaved forms of other heathers. Its insignificant flowers are produced in April.

Erica terminalis (*E. stricta*), Corsican heath, is a native of the western Mediterranean, and is naturalised in Ireland. It is hardier than might be expected with such a home. Its habit is upright, up to 4 to 8 feet (1.2–2.4 m). The pale rose flowers last over a long period from June to October. It is distinct in its habit from all other tall-growing heaths and the old stems with their gnarled growth as seen in Bodnant Gardens have a peculiar charm of their own.

The Corsican heath *Erica terminalis*, flowering in the summer and autumn

In the chalk garden so skilfully planted at Highdown near Worthing in Sussex by the late Sir Frederick Stern, I have seen seedlings growing from self-sown seeds on what is almost wholly chalky soil. I derive much pleasure from the attractive russet coloured dead flowers in the winter months, but find there is considerable repair work to be done to the branches after a snowfall.

Erica tetralix, cross–leaved heath, is native in northern and western Europe. It makes a small shrub up to 9 inches tall (22 cm). The dark green leaves are arranged in fours round the stem forming a cross. The rose coloured flowers are produced from June to October.

Erica vagans, Cornish heath, grows wild in south west Europe and Cornwall. It is a straggling shrub, forming a bush up to 2½ feet high (75 cm) and 4 feet across (1.2 m). The bell-shaped flowers are usually pale purplish pink with protruding stamens, produced from July to November.

HYBRIDS

There are five hybrids known between species of hardy *Erica*. None in the trade are the result of deliberate crosses and all are almost completely sterile.

E. × darleyensis (*E. carnea* × *E. erigena*) was first noticed at the end of the last century at Darley Dale, Derbyshire. It is a neat shrub intermediate between its parents, and selections are listed on pp. 49 and 66.

E. × stuartii (*praegeri*) (*E. mackayana* × *E. tetralix*). The parents are closely related and the hybrid is not easy to identify. It is quite common in Ireland, but unknown in Spain.

E. × watsonii (*E. ciliaris* × *E. tetralix*). This is intermediate between its parents, flowering from July onwards. It is to be found in Cornwall, Dorset and western France.

E. × williamsii (*E. tetralix* × *E. vagans*). Found ten times on the Lizard peninsula of Cornwall and nowhere else. It flowers from August onwards. All these four hybrids have the added

Above: *Erica × darleyensis*, one of the natural hybrids between hardy *Erica* species
Below: (left) 'Exeter', a selection of *Erica × veitchii*, which is a hybrid between the tree and Portuguese heaths, and (right) the dwarf *Daboecia × scotica*, another natural hybrid

distinction that their young shoots are bright yellow, gold, pink or even red.

E. × veitchii (*E. arborea × E. lusitanica*). This has been noticed only three times and always in gardens, for the parents rarely grow near each other in the wild. Curiously, these three are somewhat more tender than their parents.

The only other hybrid among our heathers is *Daboecia × scotica* (*D. azorica × D. cantabrica*). This is larger than the first parent and smaller than the second and is hardier than both. It originated in Scottish gardens, hence its name (see also p. 58).

CULTIVARS

There are hundreds of cultivars from which to choose for the garden, and many are available from nurserymen. The main list below contains those which have had their value acknowledged by an Award of Garden Merit (AGM), the premier award given by the R.H.S. to plants known to be of garden value throughout the British Isles.

The list is divided into three groups:
A. Winter and spring flowering (p. 49).
B. Summer flowering (p. 52).
C. Foliage effect (p. 63).
The numbers in brackets after the cultivar name are measurements of height and, where possible, spread. The second figure, for spread, gives an indication of the plant spacing to use. These measurements were made from four-to-six-year-old plants in the trials and some further growth can be expected, although it will slow down with increasing age. However, plants left for many years can grow to a much greater size than is suggested from the figures below.

Winter and spring flowering

Erica × darleyensis (see p. 46)

Arthur Johnson This is clearly distinguished by its long spikes of deep pink flowers up to 9 inches (23 cm) produced from November to May. (AGM)

Darley Dale (2 ft; 60 cm) has been planted in large quantities and is one of the most attractive and reliable of all winter flowering heaths. It is very vigorous and will tolerate limey soil. It produces masses of pale pinkish mauve flowers from December to March. I know of no heath which will grow so well in difficult conditions. (AGM)

Furzey (18 × 18 ins; 45 × 45 cm). Foliage very dark green, tinged and lightly tipped red. Flowers reddish purple, from February. (AGM)

George Rendall (14 ins; 35 cm). A smaller 'Darley Dale' with deeper pinkish purple flowers from February. In spring and early summer the leaves are tinged creamy-pink at the tips.

J. W. Porter (1 × 2 ft; 30 × 60 cm). A rounded bush with red-purple flowers from February and dark green foliage. Spring foliage is bright cream and red. (AGM)

Silberschmelze ('Molten Silver') (15 × 16 ins; 38 × 40 cm). This is also mistranslated as 'Silver Beads', 'Silver Bells', 'Silver Mist'. Winter foliage dark green. Flowers white, sometimes very slightly tipped pale pink, from January.

Erica erigena (E. mediterranea)

Irish Dusk (2 ft; 60 cm). Dark foliage and salmon pink flowers from October to May. (AGM)

Golden Lady (12 ins; 30 cm). Golden yellow foliage throughout the year. White flowers in May. Slow growing. (AGM)

Superba (6 ft; 1.8 m). Free flowering with bright purplish pink flowers from March to May.

W. T. Rackliff (2 ft; 60 cm). The best white *erigena* cultivar. A compact hardy plant, with white flowers from February to May.(AGM)

Erica carnea

Adrienne Duncan (9 × 10 in; 22 × 25 cm). A beautiful plant with

very dark, bronze-green leaves and glowing crimson flowers. Rather similar to 'Vivellii', but a stronger plant. Flowers from late January to April. (AGM)

Alan Coates (5 × 13 ins; 12 × 32 cm). Foliage dull bluish green. Flowers rose-purple, from mid-February.

Ann Sparkes (3½ × 14 ins; 9 × 35 cm). Foliage bright green at base changing to green tipped with yellow. Flowers reddish purple, from February. (AGM)

Cecilia M. Beale (6 × 9 ins; 15 × 22 cm). White flowers, January to March. Compact growth with erect flowering shoots.

December Red (7 × 17 ins; 18 × 42 cm). Foliage dark, dull slightly bluish green. Flowers cyclamen purple, from late November.

Eileen Porter (9 ins; 22 cm). Rich carmine-red flowers, October to April. A seedling from 'Praecox Rubra'.

Heathwood (6 × 14 ins; 15 × 35 cm). Deep pink flowers produced from January to April. Vigorous growth with dark bluish green foliage.

King George (6 × 12 ins; 15 × 30 cm). Compact growth, dark green foliage. Flowers deep rose pink, December to April.

Loughrigg (4 × 11 ins; 10 × 27 cm). Foliage dark bluish green. Flowers rosy purple, from early February. (AGM)

March Seedling (6 × 20 ins; 15 × 50 cm). Purplish pink flowers February to April. Spreading habit.

Myretoun Ruby (6 × 18 ins; 15 × 45 cm). Dark green foliage, glowing ruby red flowers from February to April. (AGM)

Pink Spangles (6 × 20 ins; 15 × 50 cm). Foliage dark green, lighter at tips. Flowers reddish purple, from January. (AGM)

Pirbright Rose (8 × 16 ins; 20 × 40 cm). Foliage dull, dark bluish green tinged red here and there. Flowers reddish purple, from December.

Above: (left) *Erica* x *darleyensis* 'George Rendall' is smaller than the well-known 'Darley Dale', with deeper-coloured flowers (see p. 49) and (right) *Erica erigena* 'Irish Dusk', which flowers throughout winter and spring (see p. 49)
Below: (left) Two winter-flowering cultivars of *Erica carnea*, 'Ann Sparkes' set off by 'Springwood White' (see pp. 51 and 52) and (right) The brilliant spring-flowering *Erica carnea* 'Myretoun Ruby'

Praecox Rubra (10 × 22 ins; 25 × 55 cm). Foliage dull medium to dark green. Flowers rosy red, from mid-January. (AGM)

R. B. Cooke (6 × 18 ins; 15 × 45 cm). Mid-green foliage, and lavender coloured flowers, from December to May.

Ruby Glow (6 × 20 ins; 15 × 50 cm). Foliage dull dark green. Flowers pale mauve ageing to reddish purple, from late January.

Springwood Pink (6 × 13 ins; 15 × 32 cm). Foliage deep green. Flowers rose pink, from mid-January.

Springwood White (6 × 18 ins; 15 × 45 cm). Foliage dark green. Flowers white, from early February. (AGM)

Sunshine Rambler (6 ins; 15 cm). A very good yellow foliage plant, which keeps its colour throughout the year. It has a spreading habit and the young shoots are golden yellow. Flowers pink to pale pink. (AGM)

Vivellii (6 × 12 ins; 15 × 30 cm). Foliage dark green, changing to bronze in winter. Carmine-red flowers deepening at tips, from late January. (AGM)

Erica lusitanica

George Hunt (18 × 28 ins; 45 × 70 cm). Golden foliage in winter, slightly greener in summer. White flowers borne from March to April.

Summer flowering

Calluna vulgaris

Alba Jae (15 × 12 ins; 38 × 30 cm). Foliage bright medium green. Flowers white, from early August.

Alba Plena (12 × 12 ins; 30 × 30 cm). Foliage medium green. Double white flowers from mid-August.

Alba Rigida (6 × 12 ins; 15 × 30 cm). Foliage bright medium green. Single white flowers from mid-July.

Alportii (24 × 18 ins; 60 × 45 cm). Foliage dark green. Flowers bright crimson-purple, August and September.

Annemarie (15 ins; 38 cm). A compact plant, with dark foliage and double flowers opening light pink and deepening to dark pink. (AGM)

Applecross (2 ft 6 ins; 60 cm). A double pink-flowered cultivar with greyish foliage. Similar to 'H. E. Beale' (see p. 55), but the long flowering stems are taller. It keeps its foliage colour better during the winter than the 'H. E. Beale' group of cultivars. Flowers late August to October.

August Beauty (20 × 12 ins; 50 × 30 cm). Foliage fairly dark green. Flowers white, from end of July.

Aurea (12 × 10 ins; 30 × 25 cm). Foliage medium green to golden. Flowers single, purple, from end July.

Barnett Anley (18 × 12 ins; 45 × 30 cm). Foliage bright, fairly dark green. Single petunia-purple flowers in thick spikes, from mid-August.

Beechwood Crimson (18 ins; 45 cm). Deep crimson flowers from August to September.

Beoley Gold (20 × 24 ins; 50 × 60 cm). Summer foliage light green, flushed gold and pale cream. Single white flowers from mid-August. (AGM)

C. W. Nix (18 × 18 ins; 45 × 45 cm). Foliage dark dull green. Single magenta-rose flowers from early August. (AGM)

Caerketton White (18 ins; 45 cm). Rather spreading habit. Foliage has light green tips. White flowers from June to July.

County Wicklow (12 × 12 ins; 30 × 30 cm). Foliage dark green. Double pink flowers, from late July. (AGM)

Cramond (15 × 36 ins; 38 × 90 cm). Foliage very dark green. Double flowers, reddish purple to purple fading almost to white on inner petals of some sprays, from early August.

Darkness (12 × 12 ins; 30 × 30 cm). Compact habit, dark green foliage, bright crimson flowers. August to September.

Drum-Ra (12 × 12 ins; 30 × 30 cm). Foliage medium green. Flowers single white, from early August.

Elsie Purnell (20 × 20 ins; 50 × 50 cm). Foliage greyish green. Flowers double rose pink, from mid-August. (AGM)

Fred J. Chapple (15 × 12 ins; 38 × 30 cm). Foliage for most of the year medium green, but in spring it has shades of green, gold, coral pink, and copper, and the tips are purplish red. Flowers single, purple, from mid-August.

Hammondii (30 ins; 75 cm). Dark green foliage and long spikes of single white flowers in August and September. Good for cutting.

H. E. Beale (24 ins; 60 cm). Foliage greyish green which tends to 'brown' in the winter, but recovers in the spring. Flowers double, silvery pink, from September to November. Good as a cut flower.

J. H. Hamilton (8 × 12 ins; 20 × 30 cm). Foliage dark green. Flowers from early August. Double, fuchsia-pink. (AGM)

Joy Vanstone (14 × 28 ins; 35 × 70 cm). Foliage bright green at base of shoots, changing to lemon yellow on upper portions. Flowers single reddish purple, from mid-August. (AGM)

Kinlochruel (12 × 9 ins; 30 × 22 cm). A double white-flowered sport from 'County Wicklow'. Flowering July/August. (AGM)

Mair's Variety (24 ins; 60 cm). Foliage medium green. Flowers single, white, from late July. Very good for cutting as a 'white heather'. (AGM)

Mullion (10 × 10 ins; 25 × 25 cm). Foliage medium green. Flowers single, orchid-purple, from mid-August. (AGM)

My Dream (12 × 15 ins; 30 × 37 cm). A double white sport from 'H. E. Beale'. Upright growth. September to November.

Oxshott Common (30 × 30 ins; 75 × 75 cm). Foliage dull greyish green. Single purple flowers from mid-August.

Peter Sparkes (18 × 18 ins; 45 × 45 cm). A sport from 'H. E. Beale'. Flowers cyclamen purple, fading with age, from mid-August to October.

Pygmaea (5 × 8 ins; 12 × 20 cm). Foliage bright medium green. Flowers single, orchid-purple, from mid-August.

Radnor (10 × 18 ins; 25 × 45 cm). Foliage bright dark green. Flowers double reddish purple, flushed white at the base; from August. (AGM)

Rosalind (10 × 14 ins; 25 × 35 cm). Foliage yellowish green. Single mallow-purple flowers, from late August.

Above: (left) 'Beoley Gold' and (right) 'Cramond', two award-winning cultivars of *Calluna vulgaris* (see p. 53)
Below: *Calluna vulgaris* 'H. E. Beale', a good cut flower

Serlei (36 × 24 ins; 90 × 60 cm). Foliage bright medium green. Single white flowers, from late August, continuing well into the autumn.

Serlei Aurea (24 × 24 ins; 60 × 60 cm). Foliage bright greenish yellow. Single white flowers, from late August. (AGM)

Silver Rose (16 ins; 40 cm). Silver grey foliage and single bright pink flowers from August.

Sir John Charrington (15 × 18 ins; 38 × 60 cm). Foliage golden-yellow, tinged scarlet and green on upper surfaces, under surfaces bright green. Single purple flowers from August. (AGM)

Sister Anne (4 ins; 10 cm). Compact growth with silver-grey foliage, and pink flowers produced in August-September. (AGM)

Spring Cream (see p. 65).

Spring Glow (see p. 65).

Tib (10 × 12 ins; 25 × 32 cm). Foliage dark green. Double cyclamen purple flowers from late July. (AGM)

Underwoodii (15 × 15 ins; 38 × 38 cm). Foliage medium to dark green. Clusters of single silver-pink to purple flower buds are produced, which do not open into flowers. They are effective from late August over a long period and undergo changes of colour as they age, remaining whitish at the base. A very unusual plant. (AGM)

White Lawn (2 ins; 5 cm). A completely prostrate form with emerald green foliage and white flowers borne on long horizontal racemes. The plants make a neat ground-hugging mat and are very suitable for a rock garden. (AGM)

Daboecia

Alba is the name given to several white-flowered forms of *D. cantabrica* listed by nurserymen. The growth is similar to that of *D. cantabrica* but the foliage is paler and the flowers are larger.

Above: (left) The summer-flowering *Calluna vulgaris* 'Silver Rose' and (right) *Calluna vulgaris* 'Tib' produces its double flowers from late summer
Below: 'Praegerae', a delightful cultivar of *Daboecia cantabrica* (see p. 58)

Atropurpurea, another selected form of *D. cantabrica*, rich purple flowers.

Bicolor. This curious plant bears purple and white flowers and others are partly white and partly purple on the same stem. (AGM)

David Moss (12 × 18 ins; 30 × 45 cm). Foliage dark glossy green. White flowers from June. (AGM)

Praegerae (12 × 4 ins; 30 × 60 cm). Foliage bright medium green. Flowers deep pink to lighter salmon pink, from end of May. This is one of my favourites, but I have not found it so hardy as other forms of *D. cantabrica*.

Purpurea (18 × 23 ins; 45 × 57 cm). Foliage bright, medium dark green. Flower reddish purple at the base changing to purple towards the mouth, buds deep purple, from June.

Snowdrift (13 × 21 ins; 32 × 52 cm). Foliage bright green. White flowers from early June.

William Buchanan (*Daboecia × scotica*) (12 × 18 ins; 30 × 45 cm). Foliage dark glossy green. Flowers reddish purple, flowers from mid-June. (AGM)

Erica ciliaris

Corfe Castle (12 × 12 ins; 30 × 30 cm). A compact grower with clear pink flowers. July to October. (AGM)

David McClintock (15 × 12 ins; 37 × 30 cm). Light grey foliage, white flowers, deep pink tips. July/October. (AGM)

Mrs C. H. Gill (12 ins; 30 cm). Foliage dark green, compact and bushy habit. Red flowers from July to October. (AGM)

Stoborough (24 × 18 ins; 60 × 45 cm). Pearly white flowers, bright green foliage. July/October. (AGM)

Erica cinerea

Alba Minor (7 × 14 ins; 17 × 34 cm). Foliage dark dull green. Single white flowers from early June. (AGM)

Atrosanguinea Smith's Variety (8 × 20 ins; 20 × 50 cm). Foliage dark bluish green, young shoots bright green. Single reddish purple flowers from mid-June.

Cairn Valley (8 × 18 ins; 20 × 45 cm). Foliage dark green. Reddish purple flowers fading almost to white in places, from mid-June.

C. D. Eason (14 × 18 ins; 35 × 45 cm). Foliage very dark dull green. Bright rosy-red flowers from early June. (AGM)

C. G. Best (12 ins; 30 cm). Long upright spikes of salmon-pink flowers produced from June to September. (AGM)

Cevennes (12 × 14 ins; 30 × 35 cm). Foliage bright light green. Purple flowers from late June. (AGM)

Cindy (12 ins; 30 cm). Bronze-green foliage, and purple flowers produced from July to September. (AGM)

Duncan Fraser (10 × 22 ins; 25 × 55 cm). Summer foliage dark green with young tips light green. Flowers white, tinged pink, from mid-June.

Eden Valley (10 × 22 ins; 20 × 55 cm). Foliage dark fairly glossy green. Flowers white tipped phlox-purple from early June. (AGM)

Fiddler's Gold (10 × 12 ins; 25 × 30 cm). Foliage light green, young shoots green flushed yellow and red. Flowers single, purple, from early June. (AGM)

Glasnevin Red (10 × 19 ins; 25 × 47 cm). Foliage dark green. Flowers reddish purple, from early June.

Hookstone White (12 ins; 30 cm). Bright green foliage and long spikes of large white flowers. (AGM)

Knap Hill Pink (10 × 14 ins; 25 × 35 cm). Foliage very dark dull green. Flowers rich pinkish purple, from early June. (AGM)

Lavender Lady (8 × 23 ins; 20 × 58 cm). Foliage dark green. Flowers violet-purple, from mid-June.

P. S. Patrick (14 × 20 ins; 35 × 50 cm). Foliage dark glossy green, tips of shoots tinged dark purplish red. Flowers, bright reddish purple, from mid-June. (AGM)

Pentreath (9 × 18 ins; 22 × 45 cm). Foliage dark green. Flowers rich purple, from mid-June. (AGM)

Pink Foam (12 × 17 ins; 30 × 42 cm). Foliage dark green. Flowers whitish tinged mauve-pink, from mid-June.

Pink Ice (6 × 16 ins; 15 × 40 cm). Foliage bright, very dark green, tinted bronze in late winter and early spring. Flowers pink, from mid-June. (AGM)

Plummer's Seedling (12 × 16 ins; 30 × 40 cm). Foliage dark green. Flowers rich reddish purple, from mid-June.

Rosea (9 × 26 ins; 22 × 65 cm). Foliage dark green. Flowers bright rose, from early June.

Stephen Davis (8 × 15 ins; 20 × 40 cm). Foliage dark green. Flowers reddish purple, from mid-June. (AGM)

Tilford (12 × 23 ins; 30 × 57 cm). Foliage medium dark glossy green. Flowers purple, from mid-June.

Velvet Night (9 ins; 22 cm). One of the darkest-flowered cultivars available. Very deep purple flowers from June to August. (AGM)

Vivienne Patricia (11 × 17 ins; 27 × 42 cm). Summer foliage very dark green with tips of shoots and stems of branchlets tinged dark red. Flowers purple, from mid-June.

Erica mackayana

Dr Ronald Gray (6 ins; 15 cm). White flowers, borne from July to September.

Plena (6 ins; 15 cm). A low-growing plant with a spreading habit. Produces very attractive double rosy-white flowers in July and August.

Erica × stuartii (E. × praegeri)

Irish Lemon (12 ins; 25 cm). A compact plant, in which the new spring foliage is a bright clear lemon, which changes in summer to green. Erect habit and pale purple. (AGM)

Erica tetralix

Alba Mollis (9 × 9 ins; 22 × 22 cm). White flowers, silvery-grey foliage turning green with age. July to September. (AGM)

Con Underwood (9 × 9 ins; 22 × 22 cm). Large crimson flowers, grey-green foliage. June to October. (AGM)

Pink Star (9 × 9 ins; 22 × 22 cm). Pink flowers, soft grey foliage. June to October. (AGM)

Above: (left) *Erica cinerea* 'Fiddler's Gold' and (right) 'Knap Hill Pink', both flowering from early June (see p. 59)
Below: (left) 'Alba Mollis', a white-flowered cultivar of the cross-leaved heath *Erica textralix* and (right) *Erica vagans* 'Mrs D. F. Maxwell', a beautiful cultivar of the Cornish heath (see p. 62)

Erica vagans

Cream (24 × 30 ins; 60 × 75 cm). Foliage dark dull green, young shoots brighter green. Flowers white, with bright red anthers when young changing to reddish brown, faint touch of pink at tips of buds, from late July.

Diana Hornibrook (15 × 12 ins; 38 × 30 cm). Foliage dark green, young foliage bright green. Flowers crimson, from end of July.

Holden Pink (18 × 19 ins; 45 × 47 cm). Foliage dark dull green. Flowers almost white flushed mallow-purple towards tips, from mid-July.

Kevernensis Alba (15 × 22 ins; 37 × 55 cm). Foliage dark green. Flowers white with bright brown stamens, from late July. (AGM)

Lyonesse (18 ins; 45 cm). The best white, with most attractive brown anthers. (AGM)

Mrs D. F. Maxwell (12 × 20 ins; 30 × 50 cm). Foliage dark dull green with bright green tips. Flowers deep cerise with dark brown anthers, from early July. One of the finest heathers in cultivation. (AGM)

St. Keverne (11 × 20 ins; 28 × 50 cm). Foliage dark green with brighter green tips. Flowers bright rose-cerise, tinged white towards the base, dark chocolate brown anthers, from mid-July.

Erica × watsonii

Cherry Turpin (12 ins; 30 cm). This hybrid resembles *E. ciliaris* more than its other parent (*E. tetralix*), in having long racemes of pale pink flowers, rising from greyish green foliage. It has a long flowering period from July to the end of September.

Dawn (9 ins; 22 cm). Young foliage has orange-yellow tips. Rose-pink flowers produced from June to October. (AGM)

Erica × williamsii

Gwavas (8 ins; 20 cm) is a good garden plant with golden yellow tips to the young leaves, and pale pink flowers from July to October.

P. D. Williams (18 ins; 45 cm). The young leaves are yellowish green, darkening with age. Pink bell-shaped flowers are borne from July to October. (AGM)

For foliage effect

Several plants are valued for their coloured foliage, and a number have received awards as foliage plants.

Calluna vulgaris

Anthony Davis (15 × 18 ins; 38 × 45 cm). Grey-green foliage, and white flowers are borne in August-September. (AGM)

Beoley Gold (see p. 53).

Carole Chapman (15 × 15 ins; 38 × 38 cm). Foliage light green at base of shoots, pale yellow or golden yellow on upper portion of shoots, green on undersides. Single white flowers from end of July. (AGM)

Gold Haze (18 × 10 ins; 45 × 25 cm). Foliage bright golden yellow. Single white flowers from early August. (AGM)

Golden Carpet (5 × 24 ins; 12 × 60 cm). Foliage cream, tipped golden yellow, upper surface green, stems dull red. Flowers reddish purple, from early August.

Golden Feather (15 × 24 ins; 38 × 60 cm). Foliage golden-yellow, with light green showing through and tipped dark red. Single mauve flowers from late August.

Hirsuta Typica (18 × 24 ins; 45 × 60 cm). Foliage greyish green, sometimes giving the impression of silver. Single purple flowers from mid-August.

Humpty Dumpty (6 × 9 ins; 15 × 22 cm). Hummock-like growth, resembling some dwarf conifers. White flowers borne in August-September. Rather shy flowering.

Joy Vanstone (see p. 55).

Multicolor (6 × 12 ins; 15 × 30 cm). Foliage yellowish green, tipped golden and coral, but readily reverts to green. Single purple flowers, from late July.

Oxshott Common (see p. 55).

Rannoch (12 × 17 ins; 30 × 42 cm). Foliage light green on basal growths, upper part of shoots golden flushed bright red, light green on undersides. Stems on young shoots deep pink. Single purple flowers are produced from late July.

Robert Chapman (10 × 14 ins; 25 × 35 cm). Foliage in winter medium green overlaid orange-red to scarlet-red. Single rose purple flowers from mid-August. Plant for winter effect. (AGM)

Rosalind (see p. 55).

Serlei Aurea (see p. 56).

Silver Queen (6 × 9 ins; 15 × 22 cm). Silver-grey foliage, and mauve flowers produced in August-September.

Sir John Charrington (see p. 56).

Sister Anne (see p. 56).

Spring Cream (18 ins; 45 cm). Cream tipped foliage in spring, white flowers produced in August-September. (AGM)

Spring Glow (18 ins; 45 cm). The chief value of this cultivar is the colour of the young spring growth – a rich mixture of golden yellow and deep flame-coloured orange, rising from dark green shoots. It is a strong-growing plant with thick foliage. The flowers, in August and September, are an attractive mauve.

Sunset (15 × 26 ins; 37 × 65 cm). Undersides of shoots light bright green tipped yellow, upper sides tipped and tinged red, also tinged creamy yellow and orange. Produces a few pink flowers in August and September. Good as a winter foliage plant.

Erica ciliaris

Aurea (9 ins; 22 cm). Golden yellow foliage, with pink flowers in July-August. Not a robust grower.

Erica cinerea

Fiddler's Gold (see p. 59).

Golden Drop (6 × 9 ins; 15 × 22 cm). Copper coloured foliage in summer turning to reddish in winter. Pink flowers produced from June to August.

Above: (left) *Calluna vulgaris* 'Gold Haze' and (right) 'Golden Feather', two heathers with excellent foliage effect (see p. 63)
Below: (left) The striking winter foliage of *Calluna vulgaris* 'Robert Chapman' and (right) *Erica carnea* 'Foxhollow', valuable for its summer and winter foliage (see p. 66)

Golden Hue (12 ins; 30 cm). Golden summer foliage changing to red as winter approaches. Pink flowers produced from June to August. (AGM)

Windlebrooke (8 × 10 ins; 20 × 25 cm). Light golden-yellow foliage in summer turning to orange red in winter. Purple flowers. July to September. (AGM)

E. × darleyensis

Jack H. Brummage (10 × 12 ins; 25 × 30 cm). Foliage bright light green, young shoots golden yellow, green at tips with bright red stems. Reddish purple flowers with dark chocolate brown stamens from mid-November.

Erica erigenea

Golden Lady (see p. 49).

Erica carnea

Ann Sparkes (see p. 51).

Aurea (8 × 24 ins; 20 × 60 cm). Foliage bright green and lemon yellow, some shoots flushed pink at the tips. Deep pink flowers from January to April.

Foxhollow (9 ins; 22 cm). Foliage golden yellow in summer, turning to deep gold, flecked red, in winter. Pale pink flowers.

Sunshine Rambler (see p. 52).

Erica vagans

Valerie Proudley (6 × 13 ins; 15 × 32 cm). Foliage bright lemon yellow throughout the year. A few white flowers from early September. (AGM)

Shrubs to Use
in the Heather Garden

In most established heather gardens, very effective use can be made of either single specimen shrubs which have been carefully sited, or groups of a kind which either blend or contrast with the planting scheme. The choice is wide and the selection need not be restricted to the Erica family.

I have seen very good use made of the following:

Acer palmatum 'Dissectum' and 'Dissectum Atropurpureum'. These are dense growing Japanese maples which form rounded, slow growing bushes with fine divided leaves, particularly beautiful in spring and autumn. To be planted as single specimens.

Andromeda polifolia, bog rosemary. A dwarf shrub of the Erica family with narrow glaucous leaves having a white under-surface. The soft pink, pitcher-shaped flowers are borne in terminal racemes in May.

Arctostaphylos uva-ursi, bearberry. A trailing evergreen with white to pink clusters of pitcher-shaped flowers in June.

Berberis. There are a few small-growing berberis, both deciduous and evergreen, which are effective. Among these are *B. thunbergii* 'Atropurpurea Nana' and *B. wilsoniae*, both of which are deciduous; and *B. candidula*, *B. × stenophylla* 'Coccinea' and 'Corallina Compacta' and *B. verruculosa*, all of which are evergreen.

Bruckenthalia spiculifolia, Balkan heather. A dwarf heath-like evergreen with terminal racemes of rose-pink bell-shaped flowers from June.

Cytisus. Three useful brooms are *C. × beanii*, dwarf with yellow flowers; *C. × praecox*, creamy flowers in May, and *C.* 'Allgold', with rich yellow flowers also in May.

× Gaulnettya wisleyensis 'Wisley Pearl'. A small evergreen shrub which is a hybrid between *Gaultheria shallon* and *Pernettya mucronata*. It is of value in autumn and winter when it bears heavy crops of large ox-blood red fruits.

Gaultheria. *G. hispida* is a low growing evergreen with white flowers followed by most attractive white fruits. *G. miqueliana* has white flowers followed by white or pink fruits.

G. procumbens is an evergreen carpeter, particularly attractive in autumn and winter when it bears bright red fruits. *G. mucronata* (*Pernettya mucronata*) is a vigorous evergreen with dark leaves with spiny tips. In May and June the white heath-like flowers are borne in great profusion, but as male and female flowers are borne on different plants it is necessary to include male plants in the groups to ensure good crops of berries. Nurserymen usually keep stocks of these separated from the fruiting forms. There are numerous named cultivars; 'White Pearl' and 'Bell's Seedling' are two of the best.

Kalmia angustifolia. An evergreen shrub which tends to spread by underground stems. Rosy red flowers in June.

Ledum groenlandicum (Labrador tea). A very hardy evergreen with terminal clusters of white flowers from April to June.

Leiophyllum buxifolium. A neat growing evergreen shrub about 12 inches high (30 cm), with lovely pink flower buds which open to white in May and June. This makes a most attractive 'drift' in a heather garden and is one of my favourites.

Leucothoe fontanesiana 'Nana'. This is the dwarf form of the species and is a real asset to give foliage contrast among heathers. Its leathery green leaves take on bronze-purple tints in autumn and winter. The white flowers are borne in pendent racemes in spring.

Menziesia ciliicalyx. A small deciduous shrub of the Erica family which always attracts attention, both for its hairy leaves and cream to soft purple flowers in May. The variety *purpurea* has rose-purple flowers.

Rhododendron. I feel that if any rhododendrons are included they should not detract from the heathers, for there could be a tendency to be looking at rhododendrons with heathers among them, rather than the reverse. The rhododendron that I would plant first and foremost is the dwarf form of *Rhododendron racemosum*, 'Forrest's Dwarf', still propagated under Forrest's collecting number 19404, which grows to about 2 feet (60 cm); the flowers are bright pink, borne in clusters along the shoots. 'Fittra' (mallow purple flowers) and 'Spinulosum' (apricot pink) are two hybrids of *R. racemosum* that also suit the heather garden.

Above: *Acer palmatum* 'Dissectum' and, below (left), *Gaultheria procumbens* are two shrubs which associate particularly well with heathers (see p. 67)
Below: (right) The dwarf *Rhododendron ferrugineum*, a European native

Other rhododendrons I would choose are R. *ferrugineum* – up to 4 feet (1.2m), tubular rosy crimson flowers; R. *hirsutum* – up to 4 feet (1.2 m), with rose-pink to scarlet flowers and its hybrid 'Myrtifolium' lilac pink flowers; R. *lepidostylum* – up to 3 feet (90 cm), bluish green leaves, pale yellow flowers; R. *micranthum* – up to 3 feet (90 cm), flowers milky white; R. *pubescens* – up to 4 feet (1.2 m), flowers rose to pinkish white; R. *tephropeplum* – up to 6 feet (1.8 m), flowers pink to purplish; R. *trichostomum* – up to 4 feet (1.2 m), flowers rose or white.

Sorbus reducta. A dwarf mountain ash, forming a suckering shrub from 2 to 3 feet high (60–90 cm). The leaves turn to bronze and reddish purple in the autumn, the fruits are white flushed rose. This looks very much at home as a 'clump' among heathers.

Ulex gallii. A dwarf gorse, flowering in summer and autumn. This in the smaller scale of a garden gives the effect of the common gorse in the wild setting of the moorland. Another dwarf gorse which is at its best in September, is *U. minor*. Both species are best planted in dry hungry soil conditions and I find them particularly good among *Erica cinerea* and its cultivars.

Vaccinium myrtillus. A native whortleberry and blueberry seen in quantities on our moorlands, where it forms masses of suckering angular shoots. The greenish pink flowers from April to June are followed by dark purple edible berries. This is worth growing among heathers for the effect of its slender branches alone, and I like it particularly in the winter after the leaves have fallen.

Vaccinium vitis-idaea, cowberry. Another British native plant, a dwarf creeping evergreen, with small shiny leaves and white to pink terminal racemes of bell-shaped flowers from June to August. The edible red fruits taste acid.

CONIFERS

I like to include a selection of dwarf and slow growing conifers among heathers. It is difficult to make a choice from the wealth of material available, but the following list is a selection which should suit most tastes. Very much more information will be found in the second section of this book, *Dwarf and Slow Growing Conifers*, pp. 75–133.

Upright, including conical and pyramidal forms

Chamaecyparis lawsoniana, Lawson's cypress. 'Ellwoodii' with feathery grey-green foliage, and 'Ellwood's Gold' with yellow-tinged tips to the branches. 'Minima Aurea' is conical in outline with golden yellow foliage.

Chamaecyparis obtusa. 'Nana Gracilis' is cone-shaped with dark green foliage.'Tetragona Aurea' has golden yellow foliage, and may in time grow to a small tree.

Chamaecyparis pisifera, Sawara cypress. 'Boulevard' has a conical habit, steely blue foliage, tinted purple in winter.

Chamaecyparis thyoides, white cypress. 'Andelyensis' is rather columnar in habit with dark bluish green foliage. 'Ericoides' is cone-shaped with green foliage in summer changing to bronze or plum coloured in winter.

Juniperus virginiana, pencil cedar. 'Sky Rocket' has very narrow columnar growth and blue-grey foliage.

Picea glauca. 'Albertiana Conica' is cone shaped, with dense growth with bright green foliage.

Thuja occidentalis, white cedar. 'Rheingold' is conical in habit, the rich deep foliage shaded amber, particularly effective in winter, but grows to 8 feet (2.4 m).

Thuja orientalis 'Elegantissima' is columnar in habit. Golden-yellow foliage tinged old-gold, changing to green in the winter.

Thuja plicata, western red cedar. 'Rogersii' has a conical habit, gold and bronze-coloured foliage.

Rounded or flat topped including forms which tend to spread

Abies balsamea, balsam fir. 'Hudsonia' is flat topped, with dark green foliage.

Chamaecyparis lawsoniana 'Pygmaea Argentea' of rounded habit, and dark bluish green foliage with silvery-white tips.

Cryptomeria japonica, Japanese cedar. 'Bandai-sugi' makes a compact bush which tends to become rugged with age. It has green foliage. 'Jindai-sugi' is more upright in growth, tending to spread out into a flat top, but with an attractive irregular branching habit.

Picea abies, Norway spruce. 'Gregoryana' of rounded habit, and sea green foliage; a very popular dwarf conifer.

Picea mariana, black spruce. 'Nana' has a globular habit with grey-green foliage.

Picea pungens 'Compacta' is a flat-topped blue spruce.

Pinus mugo, mountain pine, is a strong growing large shrub or small tree which is more suitable for the larger heather garden, but there are dwarf forms available.

Pinus sylvestris, Scots pine. 'Beuvronensis' is a dwarf with grey or bluish green foliage.

Thuja orientalis. 'Aurea Nana' has a globular habit with light yellow green foliage. 'Hillieri' makes a compact medium–sized bush with soft yellow green foliage changing to green in winter.

Thuja plicata 'Hillieri' is rounded in habit, with moss–like green foliage.

Thujopis dolobrata 'Nana', a spreading flat-topped form with bright green foliage, tending to take on bronze tints in winter.

Ground cover

Junipers are well suited as a ground cover to provide contrast among the heather foliage.

Juniperus communis, common juniper. 'Repanda' is a dwarf spreading juniper with green foliage tending to become slightly bronze in winter.

Juniperus conferta is prostrate growing with bright apple green foliage and a white band on the upper surface.

Juniperus sabina, savin. 'Tamariscifolia' is an old favourite, growing into a dense flat topped spreading bush with bright green foliage.

Above: *Vaccinium vitis-idaea* growing with heathers (see p. 70)
Below: (left) A group of conifers of various shapes, with *Juniperus conferta* in front
(right) *Juniperus sabina* 'Tamariscifolia' against a background of *Daboecia*

Dwarf and Slow-growing Conifers

JOHN BOND AND LYN RANDALL

Pinus strobus 'Prostrata' is a graceful spreading conifer with long needles

The popular *Chamaecyparis pisifera* 'Boulevard', an example of a slow-growing conifer which may eventually become too large (see p. 100)

Introduction

Ask the question 'What is your opinion of dwarf conifers?' among your circle of gardening friends and you will very likely receive one of the following answers: 'Weird, abnormal, certainly not for me'; 'Wonderful, exciting, an absorbing group of plants'; or, most frequently, 'But they never stay dwarf, do they?'

There is a great deal of truth in this last reply, for there are very few truly dwarf conifers, that is those attaining an ultimate height and spread of 2 by 2 feet (60 × 60 cm). There are, however, many other fine conifers which, although they will eventually reach a height of 4 to 6 feet (1.2–1.8 m) and a similar spread, will achieve these dimensions only after very many years. (Rates of growth vary according to the species and environment and it is not possible to be more precise.) It is for this reason that the title *Dwarf and Slow-growing Conifers*, rather than *Dwarf Conifers*, has been chosen for this section of the book.

The statement 'Weird, abnormal, etc.' is another fairly common comment and again it contains some truth. A few dwarf conifers do have a strange appearance, but these are a very small minority compared to the many normal forms which can be obtained.

The third answer, in favour of dwarf conifers, is the most usual reaction. There is a wealth of first-rate plants available and these can and do provide a growing number of gardeners with an absorbing hobby. In fact, be warned; if you become 'hooked' on dwarf conifers, you are in danger of having your lives, and your gardens, dominated by them.

Dwarf conifers are undoubtedly plants for today, with gardens continually shrinking in size. Great care should be taken in planting these small areas where space is at a premium and scale all important, paying particular attention to the ultimate size of the plants chosen.

It should be made clear to all readers that this book is concerned with conifers which remain naturally dwarf or slow-growing, without any artificial aid such as root pruning or root restriction in small containers. (This form of cultivation is called bonsai and is dealt with adequately in many books, including an excellent volume in this series.)

One last reminder—conifers provide us with the best of evergreens and are more than capable of holding the stage throughout the year.

Uses in the Garden

The landscape value of conifers is in no doubt. Being mostly ever-green, they add great strength of form, shelter and frequently privacy to the garden. This is particularly obvious if the garden contains a strong element of deciduous trees and shrubs. Conifers have a similar role to play, on a much larger scale, in the country-side. Because Britain is poorly endowed with native conifers—just three species, only one of which is a respec-table tree—we rely heavily on foreign introductions for forestry and general landscape purposes. Many people wish that these exotics had not been so extensively planted, particularly the vast masses of Sitka spruce which have produced such a boring land-scape in parts of the country. There is certainly a lesson for the gardener to learn from this—think very carefully about the plac-ing of your conifers and make sure that every one of them has a part in the overall design.

We are fortunate in having a range of highly ornamental species and forms of conifers, suitable for gardens of all sizes. In the 25-acre garden, for example, trees with an ultimate height of 50 to 100 feet (15–30 m) can be used safely and for the one-acre garden there are many which will fairly slowly attain 25 feet (7 m). There is no reason why the great variety of smaller conifers should not also be used in these larger gardens. However, it is in the small garden so common today that dwarf and slower-growing conifers come into their own and provide the same effect, scaled down, as their larger allies.

As already pointed out, it is very important to consider the ultimate height and spread of dwarf conifers when selecting them for specific purposes. So much of their garden value is in the form and outline, which will be completely lost if the plants are crowded or allowed to grow into one another. Even worse, branches may die and leave unsightly gaps.

One of the major concerns of modern gardeners is time and, quite understandably, slow-growing plants have little to recom-mend them when an instant garden is required. This is a particular problem in the case of dwarf conifers, since mature specimens are rarely offered by nurseries and are consequently very expensive. There is, however, a solution.

The reader will remember that we are considering true dwarf conifers with an ultimate height and spread of 2 by 2 feet (60 × 60 cm) and slow-growing forms which will eventually reach

6 by 6 feet (1.8 × 1.8 m). My suggestion is to plant some temporarily, to fill the space until the permanent plants have grown. For example, forms with an ultimate size of 4 feet (1.2 m) are planted where 2 feet (60 cm) will be required, 6 feet (1.8 m) for 4 feet (1.2 m) and 8 to 10 feet (2.4–3 m) for 6 feet (1.8 m). These 'fillers' or short-term plants are then removed when the long-term plants, already planted in their correct sites, have grown sufficiently large to create the desired effect. This plan calls for a well researched planting scheme and careful selection of both the short- and long-term plants—colour, form and ultimate size being most important. It also demands a certain toughness from the gardener when the time for removal arrives, for we are often too tender-hearted about disposing of trees and shrubs from our gardens. The short-term plants, if in good condition, could be transplanted to other areas of the garden.

The plan outlined above is probably most applicable in a fairly wide border, with room for the tallest plants at the back and the smallest at the front. Welcome irregularity can be achieved by placing a few slightly larger specimens at the front and, of course, by using some spreading forms. Shape and colour will play an important part in the overall design and you may want to introduce a few deciduous plants for contrast, which could include some with fine foliage, such as the forms of *Acer palmatum* 'Dissectum', and even roses where space allows. These would ease the heavy, somewhat stodgy general appearance of the conifers and would also provide interest and colour during the months when conifers are in a less decorative phase.

The island bed offers a most attractive setting for dwarf conifers and arguably the greatest challenge, for it must achieve perfection on all four sides. Again, contrasting plants can be used with the conifers—dwarf bulbs, thymes, a collection of campanulas, dwarf heathers—the range of suitable plants is endless. A few well chosen and carefully placed pieces of stone might add to the effect. Another idea is to associate a fine block of stone or rock with a single conifer on a lawn, to provide an eye-catching feature. It should be emphasized that there are numerous dwarf and slow-growing conifers for a border or island bed of any size and that an area of a few square feet or considerably larger will be equally exciting to plant.

Dwarf conifers are invariably regarded as ideal for the rock garden, but only certain kinds are appropriate. It is better to choose those of prostrate or irregular and windswept appearance, and then only if they are very slow to develop, and to avoid those of regular and perfect outline—unless you want to create a setting for gnomes!

Heathers associate particularly well with dwarf conifers to provide interest throughout the year

The heather garden offers much more scope, particularly for conifers of uneven shape like the dwarf pines. Although some people may find the association somewhat overdone for their taste, there is no doubt that a selection of heathers to flower all the year round, together with a carefully chosen range of conifers, will produce a very effective garden of reasonably low maintenance and continuous interest. Many conifers are especially valuable in winter, when they take on beautiful colours of gold, deeper gold or bronze and attractive hues of brown and purple.

Much has been written in recent times in praise of ground cover. Providing the soil is first cleared of perennial weeds,

Juniperus communis 'Hornibrookii' is well known and an ideal plant for ground cover (see p. 106)

---

labour can be greatly reduced by the close planting of ground cover, which will prevent further germination and development of weeds (see also the Wisley Handbook, *Ground Cover Plants*). Conifers, particularly the dense prostrate junipers, are excellent for this purpose, but will take at least two or three years to become fully effective. Such plants are also extremely useful for clothing and stabilizing steep banks and similar difficult sites.

So far, we have discussed the use of dwarf and slow-growing conifers in informal settings. There are many other extremely good conifers of regular, near perfect outline which lend themselves to formal situations—the two sentinels at the front door or gate, for instance, which are always popular. While very few dwarf conifers make good hedges, a large number of formal outline are suitable for low partitions or screens, which can be desirable features in their own right and are ideal for surrounding a formal or kitchen garden. Many dwarf conifers are also reliable in large containers. These should not be too small, for a larger amount of soil will ensure a longer life for the plant in this somewhat artificial form of gardening.

The recent convert to dwarf conifers may well expect that they all come from mountainous areas and are normally dwarf in the wild. This is true of a few species, for instance *Pinus mugo* from the European Alps, *P. pumila* from Japan and *Juniperus horizontalis* from the mountains of north eastern America, which have given us numerous good dwarf forms. However, most dwarf selections have originated quite differently. These three species are reliable dwarf conifers; other natives of high mountains are less trustworthy and may produce seedlings whose dwarfing has been caused by the harsh climatic conditions (which may also occur in severe maritime exposure). If these are lifted and grown in more favourable garden conditions, they rapidly assume a normal tall stature.

So much for dwarf conifers in the wild; a more lucrative source of true dwarf forms is the nurseryman's seed bed. When thousands of seeds are sown, there is often considerable variation among the resulting seedlings, which can lead to dramatic differences in foliage, form, colour and speed of development. Similar changes can also occur among naturally regenerated seedlings and the keen enthusiast should watch out for these when walking through the forest. Not all species of conifer are equally free in producing variations of offspring. *Chamaecyparis lawsoniana* is one of the most prolific and a batch of its seedlings is likely to produce a great range of coloured and slower-growing forms.

Branch sporting, a further source of new forms including dwarf ones, is of great interest. Sports are genetically sound and distinct changes in colour or growth which occur on normal branches. When these new growths are sufficiently large, propagating material is removed and, if the resulting plants are considered distinct and worthy of garden space, a stock of new plants will be built up by the nurseryman.

The final source of dwarf conifers is perhaps the most exciting and is responsible for many of the finest forms. A number of conifers, in particular the pines, spruces and silver firs, frequently develop 'witches' brooms', which are congested, tight and gnarled bundles of small, but otherwise healthy, growths attached to normal branches. These brooms are thought to be the result of parasitic or some other pathological interference. If propagation material is removed and grafted, it will provide first-class new

A conifer garden showing an effective contrast of shapes and colours

plants, which usually remain dwarf. Of great interest is the fact that these brooms or the resulting propagations often produce diminutive cones, complete with small seeds. If these seeds are sown, many will produce new and most desirable dwarf conifers.

We would like to make a plea at this stage to anyone involved in raising new dwarf conifers. Please assess the selected plant very thoroughly before naming and releasing stock to our gardens, for we already have a wealth of plants available and anything new must be distinct and, above all, reliable and worthwhile.

JUVENILE AND ADULT FOLIAGE

All seed-raised conifers begin life with leaves of a distinctly heather-like appearance, known as juvenile foliage, which is quite different from the adult foliage developed by the plant as it matures. This juvenile foliage is occasionally held by the plant throughout its life and remains fixed when propagated vegetatively. There are many desirable dwarf conifers of this kind.

The junipers are a well known example of a genus where both types of foliage are present. Some species, like J. *communis*, retain the juvenile leaves permanently; others, such as J. *virginiana*, produce juvenile and adult leaves together. Foliage intermediate between the juvenile and adult states may also be found, as in the case of the Plumosa group of *Chamaecyparis pisifera*.

83

—— Cultivation and Propagation ——

SUITABLE CONDITIONS

Conifers will thrive in any good soil, although many are tolerant of very poor soil conditions, including the poorest peaty acid soils. The exception is soil with a high lime content or thin soil over chalk where there are serious limitations. However, we are saved by two genera, the junipers and the yews, which will succeed in limy conditions, and luckily both contain many good and useful dwarf forms. Apart from the spruces and a few others, conifers will not accept waterlogged soil.

Poor soil is not a disadvantage; in fact, it may well be advantageous, because dwarf conifers will grow and develop slowly in such a soil and will therefore assume more desirable and attractive characteristics. But poor soils are frequently dry soils and watering may be necessary to ensure that conifers do not become too dry, particularly when newly planted. Once established, however, plants should not require watering if a good mulch is applied regularly.

Mulching not only conserves moisture, but helps to restrict weed growth and make the task of weeding less irksome, for any weeds that do grow may be easily removed. It also gives an attractive finish to the surface and, if evenly applied, it will improve the appearance of all permanent plantings. The first choice of mulching material should be leafmould, either from hardwood trees such as oak or beech, or from softwood trees like pine, the latter being particularly suitable since it inevitably contains small cones and freshly fallen needles which blend well with dwarf conifers. Other sources of mulch are shredded bark, and wood chips. The mulch is best applied in winter, to form a layer with a depth of 2 or 3 inches (5–8 cm), when the soil is wet.

Organic and inorganic fertilizers should not be necessary and, if used at all, should be used only sparingly. Heavy feeding will result in fast uncharacteristic growth.

Dwarf conifers, with their compact, stocky form, are generally wind-resistant, but planting in frost pockets should be avoided. Frosts in late spring can be especially troublesome, damaging the new soft young shoots. In a severe winter, the tight close growth of certain dwarf conifers holds large quantities of water which, when frozen hard, results in whole branchlets being killed, thus

'Rigid Dwarf', like many of the very dwarf forms of *Chamaecyparis obtusa*, needs winter protection (see p. 97)

ruining the entire plant. Many of those susceptible, particularly the diminutive forms of *Chamaecyparis obtusa* and *C. pisifera*, are safer in an alpine house; alternatively, they may be protected by a pane of glass held above the plant on four sticks.

Heavy snowfall can be another problem, especially with conifers of upright growth which are forced open by the weight of the snow. A sharp knock with a broom handle should dislodge the snow and restore the branches to their natural shape.

Very few conifers are able to tolerate shade, the yews being the only exception, and this particularly applies to dwarf conifers. In fact, full exposure to light is essential to get the finest shape and colour from dwarf conifers.

CHOOSING AND PLANTING

Almost all dwarf conifers offered for sale today are grown in containers and if well developed plants are bought, there should be no difficulty in establishing them at any time of year. The best period is from October to April, when the weather is normally moister and cooler and the plants are dormant. However, planting should never be done if the soil is frozen, as the roots could be damaged.

There is a tendency with container-grown plants for the roots to encircle the base of the container. These roots should be carefully unravelled before being spread out around the area of the planting hole. Make sure that the hole is large enough to take the whole root system without crowding and place the plant in the ground only fractionally deeper than it was in the container. Then replace the soil and firm it well around the plant. The whole planting operation should be performed with great care and thoroughness, for our chosen dwarf conifers are likely to remain in the garden for many years.

If plants from the open ground (as opposed to container-grown) are acquired, perhaps from friends or transplanted from your own garden, they will need special attention in the first year after planting, for even if the plant is lifted with a good ball of soil, some roots are bound to have been damaged. Watering in dry weather will be necessary and a screen of hessian shading to provide shelter from sun and wind will help the new plant to become established. If the plant is large and perhaps has only a small root ball, it should be supported with a stake during the first year or two to reduce stress from the wind.

When selecting plants from the nursery, look for ones which are a good shape, without any unsightly holes, bare stems or dead twigs or branches. They should appear healthy and have a good colour, keeping in mind the great variation in colour and the fact that many conifers change colour when slightly starved in containers or during the winter months.

Whenever possible, choose plants on their own roots rather than grafted plants. The latter tend to be much more vigorous and may lose important characteristics because of the fast-growing species which are used as rootstocks. Most dwarf forms of Chamaecyparis, Cryptomeria, Juniperus, Picea, Taxus and Thuja are easily propagated by cuttings and should be generally available on their own roots. However, Abies, Cedrus, Cupressus, Larix, Pinus and Pseudotsuga are only very rarely offered on their own roots. These have to be grafted and will be more expensive in view of the greater expertise involved in their propagation. When selecting grafted plants, always look for a good clean union between scion and stock and ensure that there are no suckers arising from below the union.

PRUNING

The pruning of dwarf conifers is a controversial matter. Many experts recommend leaving the plants to take their own course, while others are in favour of judicious shaping and checking of

86

Dwarf conifers mingle well with alpines in a raised bed

the rank growth which unfortunately appears on some forms. If pruning is practised, it is very important not to spoil the general outline and character of the plant (a topiary-type specimen is the last thing that is wanted!).

The effects of poor soil and full exposure have already been referred to (see pp. 84 and 85). Root pruning may be used in the same way, to help slow down the rate of growth and maintain the true shape of the plant. This operation should be carried out in winter, by inserting a sharp spade to its full depth around the plant at the perimeter of the branches.

Conifers, in common with all evergreens, lose their leaves during the summer months. Many dwarf conifers hold this dead foliage among their twigs and branches which prevents light and air reaching the centre of the plant. This is particularly troublesome in the very tight-growing forms and will result in a considerable number of dead branchlets if the debris is not cleared away—a tedious but very necessary task.

PROPAGATION

Propagation of many conifers from cuttings is comparatively easy, although some can only be increased by grafting (see p. 86). Any rank strong growth at the top of the mother plant should be avoided when taking cuttings, for while this is often easier to root, it will produce plants with uncharacteristic loose growth. Short slow growth is the ideal material. Cuttings may be taken either with a heel (a piece of the main stem attached) or as firm tip growth between August and March, the optimum time being September to November, and are best inserted in a frame with bottom heat. Good results can also be obtained using a cold frame in August and September. More difficult genera, the dwarf spruces and dwarf tsugas for example, will respond more readily if placed under a mist system. A mixture of 50% peat and 50% sharp sand is the normal medium for rooting and a hormone rooting powder will improve the percentage of rooted cuttings. If a frame is used, it will be necessary to spray the cuttings with water twice daily in warm weather and to shade the frame on sunny days.

Grafting presents a greater challenge and certainly adds interest for the keen enthusiast. The task, however, calls for some skill and is outside the scope of this book. There are several specialist books on propagation which will provide all the necessary details, including *The Grafter's Handbook* by R. J. Garner (fifth edition, 1988, Cassell).

Outline shapes of dwarf conifers: 1 bun-shaped; 2 mound-shaped; 3 globose; 4 pyramidal; 5 conical; 6 columnar; 7 weeping; 8 ground-hugging; 9 prostrate; 10 semi-prostrate; 11 wide-spreading

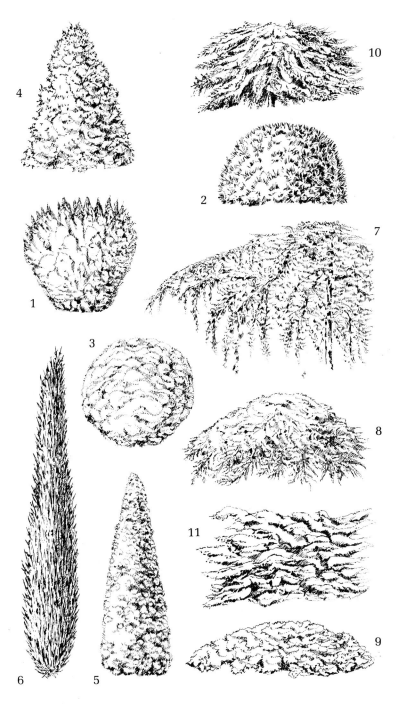

— Recommended Dwarf Conifers —

The following list is arranged in alphabetical order of genus and gives brief descriptions of some of the most worthwhile cultivars. It also includes rarer plants (indicated by an asterisk *), which are not normally available from general nurseries and garden centres, but may often be obtained from growers specializing in dwarf and slow-growing conifers.

Measurements refer to the expected height and width after ten years, unless otherwise stated. However, these are only approximate and will vary according to growing conditions.

Abies

The silver firs are some of the grandest and most beautiful trees to be seen in the wild and their native habitat extends through the northern hemisphere from North America to Europe and China. Some species have particularly attractive cones and others are strikingly colourful in spring when male and female 'flowers' appear. Regrettably, they do not lend themselves readily to producing dwarf forms, although there are a few good small and slow-growing varieties.

A. amabilis is the red silver fir from the foothills of western North America and has given rise to a superb horizontal form, 'Spreading Star'*. The silver-grey, needle-like leaves provide an attractive background for the bright red male cones in the spring. ($3\frac{1}{4} \times 5-6\frac{3}{4}$ ft; $1 \times 1.5-2$ m.)

A. balsamea, the balsam fir, is another North American native and is not tolerant of chalky soils. There are two very good dwarf forms.
'Hudsonia' has dark green foliage and forms a rounded compact bush. The needles are held semi-radially, leaving a distinct parting on the stems. It is hardy and trouble-free. ($1\frac{1}{2}$ ft; 50 cm.)
'Nana' is similar but, since the leaves are arranged all around the stems, it has a denser look.

A. cephalonica, a mountain species from Greece, is ideal for chalky soils. The only dwarf form, 'Meyer's Dwarf' (formerly called 'Nana'), is an attractive flat-topped plant. Very slow-growing and compact, it does not produce a leading shoot. (3¼ ft; 1 m.)

A. *concolor*, the Colorado white fir, is a beautiful mountain species which has produced a fine dwarf called 'Compacta', often offered under the name 'Glauca Compacta'. It is of compact but irregular growth. (3¼ ft; 1 m.)
'Pigglemee'* is a new dwarf cultivar which is worth searching for at specialist nurseries.

A. *koreana*, although not a dwarf, is included here for its slow growth and for its usefulness in the border or as a specimen plant in the larger garden. It originates from mountainous areas of Korea and has attractive foliage of glossy green with white undersides. However, the most notable feature is the blue cones, which are held upright on the branches and, unlike many other *Abies* species, produced at an early age. (9¾ ft; 3 m; see p. 92.)
'Compact Dwarf' is very small with horizontally held branches, but unfortunately no cones. (2½ ft; 70 cm.)
'Prostrate Beauty' is a procumbent form with an irregular spreading habit. Any vertical shoots that appear will have to be removed to maintain the shape. (4–6 ft; 1.2–1.8 m.)

A. *lasiocarpa*, another mountain species from North America of naturally slow growth, has given us an even slower-growing form in 'Compacta'. This is a broadly conical bush of irregular outline with attractive greyish green foliage. (Ultimately 6 ft; 1.8 m.)

A. *nordmanniana* has given rise to a delightful golden dwarf form, 'Golden Spreader', a rarity among the firs. The short prostrate branches bear bright golden yellow foliage whose colour intensifies during the winter. It is best grown in semi-shade to prevent scorching by the sun. (1 × 1½ ft; 30 × 50 cm.)

A. *procera*, aptly called the noble fir, is a native of western North America and has branches densely furnished with greyish green foliage. It will not grow well on chalk soils. A fine dwarf from is 'Glauca Prostrata', which probably originated as a side graft of the glaucous form and has bluish grey foliage. Slow-growing and of low spreading habit, it may sometimes produce vertical shoots and these should be removed before they become too dominant. (1 × 3¼ ft; 30 × 100 cm.)

Above: Foliage of *Abies*, left, and *Cedrus*, right
Below: *Abies koreana*, naturally compact and slow-growing, produces its
beautiful cones at an early age (see p. 91)

Cedrus

The cedars are a magnificent group of conifers. They adorn many parks and large gardens with their elegance and grace, although they are often planted in spaces much too small for their extensive growth.

C. brevifolia is a typical mountain species, originating from Cyprus, and tends to be variable when raised from seed. With its small needles and slow growth, it has a dwarf appearance, which can be maintained by occasional careful pruning. (4 ft; 1.2 m.)

C. deodara, the Himalayan cedar, has the longest needles of all the species and a naturally drooping habit. There are several good forms, the most popular among the trees probably being 'Aurea'. For the smaller garden, however, the low-growing 'Aurea Nana'* is becoming better known.

'Golden Horizon'* is a recent introduction of semi-prostrate habit with gracefully weeping branches $(2\frac{1}{2}$–4 ft; 80–120 cm spread.)

'Nana'* forms a low bush and is very slow-growing. The compact branches will spread much wider than high, making this a very desirable dwarf conifer. (8 × 16 in.; 20 × 40 cm.)

'Pendula' could perhaps be more aptly named 'Prostrata', as it seems to prefer to hug the ground in a tumbling mass and can be quite vigorous in its spread. Timely removal of any ascending branches will maintain the creeping habit but, if a large weeping form is required, the leading shoot should be tied to a stake when young.

'Pygmy'* is extremely slow-growing, making less than a foot (30 cm) in height in ten years and forming a tiny mound. With its striking glaucous foliage, it is a choice but very rare plant.

C. libani, the Lebanese cedar, is probably the most familiar of the cedars with its horizontal branching system and dark foliage.

'Comte de Dijon' is a very popular smaller form. It slowly becomes a dense conical bush, with branches held horizontally, and in time will grow into a substantial shrub. $(3\frac{1}{4}$ ft; 1 m.)

Selected dwarf forms have occasionally appeared in seed beds of C. libani and have been given the epithet 'Nana'. Inevitably, these will differ in some respect from each other, but they will be similar in their bushy compact habit and slow growth and are worth including in a collection.

'Sargentii' is a distinct and valuable dwarf form which, when left to sprawl over a bank or wall, shows to advantage its long

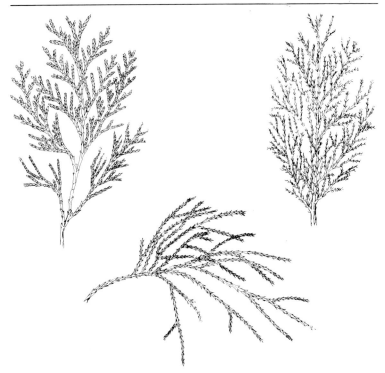

Foliage of *Chamaecyparis*: adult, left; juvenile, right; threadleaf, centre

pendulous branches. It can also be trained upwards to the height required and then allowed to display its weeping habit. (3¼ ft; 1 m.)

Chamaecyparis

This genus rates as probably the most prolific in cultivars suitable for the smaller garden. These have arisen usually as seedling variants or less often as branch sports. Of the five species hardy in Britain, three come from North America and two from Japan.

C. lawsoniana, Lawson's cypress, is well known for its usefulness as a hedging plant. It has produced a large number of extremely variable forms, from the taller-growing coloured kinds to the very dwarf ones, with many different types of foliage and shape. Most are easy to grow, preferring a moist but well-drained soil and, in the case of the yellow forms, a position in full sun to maintain the colour.

For convenience, many of the dwarf forms can be divided into groups sharing similar characteristics:

Ellwoodii group

'Ellwoodii' is widely grown and, although often offered as a dwarf, it will gain considerable height after many years. It is unrivalled among the forms with juvenile foliage, and its blue-green colour deepens in winter to a glaucous blue. Several good dwarf sports have occurred on 'Ellwoodii'.

'Chilworth Silver', also blue but of dwarfer habit, forms a fairly wide, upright, densely furnished bush.

'Ellwood's Gold' is a very attractive addition with its gold-tipped foliage and becomes a small conical bush. (4 ft; 1.1 m.)

'Ellwood's Pillar' is a miniature 'Ellwoodii' and makes a dense blue column suitable for a rock garden. (2 ft; 60 cm.)

'Ellwood's Pygmy', which is even lower-growing, is equally at home in the rock garden. It forms a rounded bun with similar blue colouring. (8 in.; 20 cm.)

'Blue Nantais' is a slow-growing conical plant of silvery blue. ($3\frac{1}{4}$ ft; 1 m.)

Minima group

'Minima', like the other forms in this group, has normal adult foliage. It is a neatly compact plant which becomes a green globose bush (2 × 2 ft; 60 × 60 cm.)

'Minima Glauca' is of the same habit and growth rate, with a bluish grey tinge to the darker foliage.

'Minima Aurea', the golden form in this group, is slightly slower in growth. Its bright colour remains constant throughout the year. ($2\frac{1}{2}$ ft; 80 cm.)

'Aurea Densa' is almost indistinguishable from 'Minima Aurea' when young, although it will eventually produce a more conical shape and is densely furnished with stiff foliage held more tightly to the plant.

'Nana' is very similar to 'Minima' but will develop a more pointed top owing to the dominant central stem, whereas the 'Minima' forms have all the branches originating from a basal stub. The foliage is held slightly more loosely than in 'Minima' and the growth rate is faster. ($2\frac{1}{2}$ ft; 80 cm.)

'Nana Glauca' is the glaucous version with blue-green foliage.

'Gimbornii' has been a favourite for many years and, although similar to 'Nana Glauca', it is more globose in shape, denser in habit and very neat in outline.

'Gnome' forms a globe-shaped plant of deep green with small closely held foliage. It often produces coarser growth, which should be pinched out at an early stage, otherwise it will take over and spoil the tight habit. It is ideal for the rock garden or small border. (1 ft; 30 cm.)

'Green Globe'* is a real miniature and one of the most compact forms, slowly becoming a tight congested bun. It is perfect for the small rock garden or even a large trough and is a seedling introduction from New Zealand. (8–12 in.; 20–30 cm.)

'Pygmaea Argentea', a popular dwarf, is prettily variegated with silver on the tops of the foliage sprays and needs to be grown in full sun to keep the variegation sharp. It is sometimes damaged by winter weather, but soon recovers in the next growing season. (3¼ ft; 1 m.)

Tamariscifolia group

'Tamariscifolia' belongs to a group of wide-spreading plants that do not form leaders and are consequently flat-topped. It has drooping sprays of light bluish green foliage. The habit is rather untidy in its young state, but eventually becomes more rounded, particularly if grown in a fully exposed situation. (2 × 4 ft; 60–120 cm.)

'Nestoides' is similar and very slow-growing, but not quite as wide-spreading.

'Nidiformis' is a very graceful cultivar, with horizontally held branches which gradually form a depression in the centre resembling a bird's nest. Its grey-green foliage has a glaucous bloom underneath. If grown in semi-shade, it will tend to be drawn upwards and lose its low-growing shape. (See below.)

C. obtusa is a Japanese species with dense dark green foliage which is distinctly blunt-ended and carried in flat sprays. It gives

Chamaecyparis lawsoniana 'Nidiformis' is distinguished from the very similar 'Tamariscifolia' by the bluntly rounded sprays of foliage

us an exciting range of dwarf conifers, a large number of which are exceptionally good for troughs and small rock gardens. So highly are they esteemed that many enthusiasts collect only *C. obtusa* cultivars.

Most of the smaller forms require protection in winter from the effects of freezing moisture, which can spoil their compact shape. Failing overhead protection in the garden, the best alternative is to grow them in pots and move them into a greenhouse or cold frame for the winter.

'Caespitosa'* is a tiny plant and much sought after. It forms a dense irregular bun with small shell-shaped sprays of foliage held tightly together and is very slow growing (4 in.; 10 cm.)

'Intermedia' grows a little faster and develops into a more pyramidal plant with slightly looser foliage. (6 in.; 15 cm.)

'Juniperoides' makes a rich green globose little plant, with the foliage held in open fan-shaped sprays. (6 in.; 15 cm.)

'Juniperoides Compacta'* is very similar in habit but more compact and closer-growing.

'Minima'* is a pygmy form with small tightly congested foliage resembling a pincushion. ($2\frac{1}{4}$ × 4 in.; 6 × 10 cm.)

'Nana' has upward-facing fans of foliage which form a rounded dense bush of irregular outline (6–8 in.; 15–20 cm.)

'Nana Aurea' is much more vigorous than 'Nana', despite its name. The typical fan-shaped foliage is golden on the outside of the plant fading to a yellowish green on the inside. ($1\frac{1}{2}$ ft; 50 cm.)

'Pygmaea' is a distinct flat-topped cultivar, with spreading branches of loose foliage and conspicuous brown stems. ($1\frac{1}{2}$ × $2\frac{1}{4}$ ft; 45 × 70 cm.)

'Pygmaea Aurescens' is even more attractive than 'Pygmaea' turning to a rich bronze colour during the winter.

'Repens' is a prostrate form with short closely held sprays of bright green. It tends to send up vertical shoots which should be pruned occasionally to keep it low. (1 × 2 ft; 30 × 60 cm.)

'Rigid Dwarf', also listed as 'Rigida' or 'Nana Rigida' by some nurseries, is an upright plant of very dark green, tight, fan-shaped foliage borne vertically. The greyish bloom on the undersides of the leaves is a distinctive feature. (1 ft; 30 cm; see p. 85.)

'Filicoides', a distinctive form with fern-like foliage, may in time grow into an upright small tree of 5 feet (1.5 m). However, careful removal of the strongest shoots will keep it within bounds as a slow-growing shrubby bush.

'Compact Fernspray' is very similar (and sometimes offered as 'Filicoides Compacta'), although the fern-like branchlets are much smaller and make a low broadly bushy plant.

'Fernspray Gold' is a fairly recent introduction from New

Zealand. A beautiful golden yellow plant, its foliage is like 'Fili-coides' and carried on slightly arching branches. (Ultimately 5 ft; 1.5 m; see opposite.)

'Chabo-Yadori', unlike the species itself, has mostly juvenile foliage, with a crisped look to the branchlets caused by a few tips of adult foliage in irregular sprays. It is an upright small bush of light green (2 ft; 60 cm.)

'Mariesii' is a very pretty dwarf splashed with yellowish white on the tips of the foliage and of loose open habit. (2 ft; 60 cm.)

'Spiralis', with its twisted sprays of foliage, has a distinctive appearance and is an excellent cultivar of upright shape and slow growth. (10 in.; 25 cm.)

'Tonia' is a prettily variegated form which arose as a sport on 'Nana Gracilis'. The white splashes occur haphazardly over the plant and it should be grown in full sun for these to develop. (1¼ ft; 40 cm.)

'Nana Gracilis' is widely available from nurseries and, although it will eventually make a substantial bush, it is not too small for planting in a border. The dark green foliage is fairly loosely held in shell-shaped sprays. (4 ft; 1.2 m.)

C. pisifera is another Japanese species, with scale-like foliage which is rather prickly to the touch. It too has given rise to many dwarf cultivars of different foliage types. Apart from the forms with normal adult foliage, these may be divided into the Filifera group, which has whipcord type branchlets; the Plumosa group, which is softer than the adult type and is intermediate between that and the next group; and the Squarrosa group, which is a semi-juvenile type and fluffier in appearance.

Normal foliage group

'Compacta', bun-shaped with wholly adult foliage of a blue-green colour in close tight sprays, is an ideal rockery plant. (1½ × 2 ft; 20 × 30 cm.)

'Compacta Variegata' is irregularly splashed with creamy white patches and flecks and is slightly looser in habit than its green counterpart. (Eventually 2 × 5 ft; 60 × 150 cm.)

'Nana' is a choice bun-shaped dwarf of dark green with a whitish bloom on the undersides of the small adult foliage. (8 × 20 in.; 20 × 50 cm.)

'Nana Aureovariegata' has more of a golden lustre all over the plant than a definite variegation and is at its best in full sun. It is a compact form which hugs the contours of the ground, increasing very slowly in width to 1 foot (30 cm) or more.

Above: *Chamaecyparis obtusa* 'Fernspray Gold', a lovely golden version of 'Filicoides'
Below: *Chamaecyparis pisifera* 'Filifera Aureovariegata' is a striking plant for a sunny situation (see p. 100)

Filifera group

'Filifera Aurea' is a golden version of the threadleaf foliage type. Low and rounded at first, it becomes a vigorous erect plant of narrow branchlets which hang gracefully downwards and is very effective in a border. (3¼ ft; 1m.)

'Filifera Aureovariegata' is a delightful form with splashes of creamy white variegation. Like others in this group, it makes a mound of weeping thread-like foliage and needs full sun to bring out the variegation. (5 ft; 1.5 m; see p. 99.)

'Filifera Nana' is an all green compact plant of low broad habit. The narrow pendulous branches look well when allowed to drape over a wall or large rock. (1 × 3¼ ft; 30 × 100 cm.)

'Sungold', a recent introduction in the Filifera group, is also golden yellow and forms a dense globose bush. (2 ft; 60 cm.)

Plumosa group

'Plumosa Aurea Compacta' is a golden form and globose in habit. Although slow-growing, it may eventually reach 5 feet (1.5 m).

'Plumosa Compressa' is the smallest of the C. pisifera forms and perfect for the small rock garden with its tiny foliage packed into a round ball. The yellowish green colouring is brighter in summer. It may occasionally produce shoots of looser foliage, which should be removed. (8 in.; 20 cm.)

'Snow' is a low bun of soft moss-like foliage which is tipped with white. It needs to be positioned with some care in the garden, for the tips will burn if exposed to full sun and cold winds, while the branches will become long and drawn in heavy shade, spoiling the compact shape. A sheltered spot in semi-shade should keep it happy. (3¼ ft; 1 m.)

Squarrosa group

'Boulevard' has outstanding silver-blue Squarrosa-type foliage and makes a neat dense pyramid. It is always a popular choice. (3¼–5 ft; 1–1.5 m; see p. 76.)

'Squarrosa Intermedia' is the most attractive of the forms in the Squarrosa group, many of which can become quite large. It has typical, but smaller, blue-grey foliage and makes a rounded bush of tightly congested leaves. Any extra-long thin shoots should be pinched out to keep the plant dense and small. (1½ ft; 50 cm.)

C. thyoides, the white cypress from western North America, bears open sprays of glaucous green foliage. In its native land it grows happily on quite wet ground, but it dislikes shallow soils over chalk.

'Andelyensis' is a compact form with mostly adult foliage,

showing some juvenile foliage on the lower part of the plant. (5–6½ ft; 1.5–2 m.)

'Andelyensis Nana' an even smaller version, forms an upright bush with a flattish top and dense, dark bluish green foliage. (3¼ ft; 1 m.)

'Rubicon'* is a little conical bush of neat compact habit, with juvenile foliage which is green in summer, turning to plum purple in winter. Fairly new in cultivation, it is a choice plant for the rock garden. (2 ft; 60 cm.)

Cryptomeria

C. *japonica* is the sole species in this genus and a very important timber tree in its native Japan. It has given rise to many named forms, mostly of Japanese origin, both large and small and sometimes with unusual foliage.

'Bandai-Sugi' is a well-known cultivar, slow-growing and full of character. As well as the long shoots of small dark green foliage, there are areas of miniature tightly congested leaves which give the plant its irregular and rugged outline. (3¼ ft; 1 m.)

'Globosa Nana' is a lovely globe-shaped form of dense habit and rich green colouring. It has normal adult foliage, with the needles spirally arranged on long drooping shoots. (3¼–5 ft; 1–1.5 m; see p. 102.)

'Kilmacurragh' makes a low, flatly globose plant, unlike the many forms with abnormal foliage which are usually quite tall. The juvenile foliage with fasciated branch tips like cockscombs is a distinctive feature. (2–3 ft; 60–75 cm.)

'Elegans Compacta', although not exactly dwarf, is a distinct cultivar, with the soft juvenile foliage presenting a mass of billowing pale green. Reasonably slow-growing, it can develop into a compact, flat-topped, upright plant of 5 ft (1.5 m).

'Lobbii Nana' bears juvenile foliage as in 'Elegans Compacta' but, since the leaves are much stiffer and shorter, it forms a denser rounded bush. With age it develops clusters of congested foliage at the tips, the whole plant turning a purplish brown in winter. (2 ft; 60 cm.)

'Vilmoriniana' is a true dwarf of dense globose habit and one of the most popular forms for rock gardens. It changes to a purplish brown in winter. (1¼ × 1¼ ft; 40 × 40 cm.)

'Jindai Sugi', another popular cultivar, is a compact dense bush of soft green which retains its colour throughout the year. Short stiff needles borne on branches both erect and slightly spreading give it a more open and regular habit than 'Bandai-Sugi'. (4 ft; 1.2 m.)

Above: Foliage of *Cryptomeria*, left, and *Cupressus*, right
Below: With its pendulous branchlets, *Cryptomeria japonica* 'Globosa Nana' makes a graceful specimen for a low wall or lawn (see p. 101)

Two more compact and dense forms of the same foliage type are 'Nana' and 'Pygmaea'. Both are almost identical in their rounded shape, except that 'Nana' remains green all year while 'Pygmaea' turns a reddish bronze in winter. (2 ft; 60 cm.)

Cupressus

There are many species of true cypress, but very few are hardy enough to be grown outside in the British Isles and even these generally fare better in the south and west than in the north.

C. *glabra* is a tall pyramidal tree of glaucous foliage from Arizona. Probably the only truly dwarf form is 'Compacta'*, which is an excellent broadly conical bush of tightly congested grey-green foliage. (1½ ft; 45 cm.)

C. *macrocarpa* is well known for its fine golden forms which, given a mild sheltered spot, will make quite large trees relatively quickly. There are two very dwarf forms with green foliage worth looking for.
   'Minima'*, with mainly juvenile foliage, forms a low, dense, rounded bush. Some longer adult branches may be produced, which should be removed. (1½–2 ft; 45–60 cm.)
   'Pygmaea'* is a miniature selection which arose as a seedling and is a rare and choice plant. The tightly compressed bun-shaped plant will make little more than 1½ feet (45 cm).

C. *sempervirens*, the Italian cypress, with its tall, dark green, narrow columns, is a familiar sight in the Mediterranean landscape, but only succeeds in the mildest areas of Britain.
   'Swane's Golden' is a particularly good, slow-growing, golden form which develops into a slender compact column. Where it is happy it may well exceed 4 feet (1.2 m) after ten years.

Juniperus

This is a large genus with a wide geographical distribution and has greatly contributed to the enhancement of gardens with its many species, forms and cultivars. Junipers are generally very hardy, coming from areas of poor soil and rigorous climate, and will thrive in hot dry situations as well as tolerating chalk soils. They vary considerably in shape, from tall, broad or narrow columns to low ground-hugging types, and also in texture, size, habit and colour. Indeed, the harsh exposed conditions of the mountainside have given rise to a large number of prostrate forms, particularly in J. *communis*. A distinctive feature of the junipers is the production of berry-like fruits and not cones.

J. communis is one of the three British native conifers and is found throughout the northern hemisphere. The dense prickly foliage makes ideal ground cover and there are many named forms.

'Compressa', everyone's ideal miniature for a trough or rock garden, is a tight grey-green column and will attain only 2 feet (60 cm) after many years. (See below.)

'Depressa Aurea' is a lovely spreading form with horizontal branches lifting slightly above the ground. The new growth in spring is a pretty yellow, changing in autumn to bronze with silvery bands on the undersides of the leaves. Planting in full sun will enhance the golden colour. (4 ft; 1.2 m spread; see opposite.)

Juniperus communis 'Compressa' is well known but susceptible to damage from wind and frost

Above: Foliage of *Juniperus*: adult, left; juvenile, right
Below: *Juniperus communis* 'Depressa Aurea' turns a beautiful bright yellow
in early summer

'Depressed Star' is a green form, with branches held closer to the ground. (4 ft; 1.2 m spread.)

'Hornibrookii' is a well-established cultivar among the ground-hugging forms. The branches lie flat and the short prickly leaves are twisted to display the white bands on top, giving the plant a silvery green appearance. (4 ft; 1.2 m spread; see p. 81.)

'Minima' is very similar to 'Hornibrookii' but with more obvious silvery bands on the larger leaves. It looks very effective trailing over rocks or a wall. (5 ft; 1.5 m.)

'Repanda' eventually becomes a low mound with dark green foliage which is soft to the touch. The radial growth from the centre of the plant results in a neat, almost circular outline and provides excellent ground cover where space is available.

Some more recent introductions of prostrate forms of *J. communis* are worth searching for, although they may not be readily available.

'Berkshire'* from North America, is slow-growing and cushion-like, which makes it suitable for more restricted areas.

'Gew Graze'*, a selection discovered in Cornwall, is similar to 'Repanda' but of slower growth and not quite so prostrate.

'Derrynane'*, an Award of Merit plant, deserves to be better known. It originally occurred in County Kerry and is a very prostrate form which produces berries freely.

J. conferta grows on sand dunes on the coasts of Japan, where the maritime exposure keeps it low and mat-forming. The sharply pointed green leaves make a dense carpet of some vigour.

Two forms introduced from North America are 'Blue Pacific'*, with a more procumbent habit and attractive blue-green needles; and 'Emerald Sea'*, a bright green colour forming a dense low mat. Both will have an eventual spread of 5 feet (1.5 m).

J. horizontalis, from North America, is probably the best species for ground cover. The many named forms come in a range of colours from grey-green to steel-blue, some of which take on a bronze hue for the winter. Most will cover an area of 3 feet (90 cm) quite rapidly, if fairly slowly at first, and occasional snipping back of the leading shoots in the early years will encourage dense growth from the main stems.

'Bar Harbor' is a thick mat of long, thin branches, greyish green turning to a mauve-purple in the winter. The colour is most pronounced when the plant is grown in full sun.

'Douglasii' is similar but more greyish in colour as the foliage is covered with a glaucous bloom. It also becomes purplish in winter.

'Emerald Spreader', a newcomer to the trade, should become very popular for its bright green foliage and dense growth.

'Glauca' is steel-blue, very prostrate and with long thin branchlets which tend to overlap in layers.

'Glomerata'* is distinctive for its short vertical shoots of dense rich green foliage. The prostrate main stems cover the ground less rapidly than in other forms.

'Grey Pearl', unlike most cultivars of *J. horizontalis*, is a dumpy little blue-green plant of wholly erect branches, which gradually becomes wider than it is high. (8–12 in.; 20–30 cm.)

'Plumosa Compacta' represents a group of forms characterized by the branches being held at an ascending angle radiating from the centre. It eventually makes a rather flat-topped thick bush and the light grey-green foliage turns purplish bronze in winter.

J. × media is the group name for hybrids between *J. chinensis* and *J. sabina*. The commonest is 'Pfitzeriana', which has great architectural value. Its wide-spreading branches are capable of covering a large area. Although most of the hybrids are too big for the small garden, there are a few that would be appropriate.

'Pfitzeriana Compacta' is a slow-growing version and forms a flat-topped compact plant with prickly foliage. ($3\frac{1}{4} \times 6\frac{1}{2}$ ft; 1 × 2 m.)

'Gold Coast' is a lovely golden form, also of low bushy habit. It is an outstanding cultivar with horizontally held branches. (3 × 4 ft; 90 × 120 cm.)

'Old Gold' appeared as a sport on the vigorous *J. × media* 'Pfitzeriana Aurea', but it is more compact and slower-growing. The golden colour persists all through the plant. It is larger than 'Gold Coast', with wider-spreading branches.

J. 'Grey Owl' should be mentioned here. Previously classified under *J. virginiana* and occasionally under *J. sabina*, it has now been established that it is a hybrid between *J. × media* 'Pfitzeriana', which gives it the low spreading habit, and *J. virginiana* 'Glauca', which provides the glaucous blue colour. It is an exceptional cultivar, ultimately a large wide-spreading shrub but slow growing. (2 × 5 ft; 60 × 150 cm.)

'Blaauw' belongs to the Plumosa group, which is quite different, with tightly congested foliage on branches growing at a more upright angle. It is blue-green and the leaves are densely held on short side branches. (4 ft; 1.2 m.)

'Globosa Cinerea' is almost identical to 'Blaauw' when young, but slightly less tall and becoming much broader with age.

'Shimpaku'*, the smallest member of the group, is much used for bonsai. Soft grey-green foliage makes a compact miniature version of the Plumosa type. (1 ft; 30 cm.)

J. procumbens is a prostrate mountain species from Japan of quite vigorous habit, sending out long branches of small greyish green leaves. (Ultimate spread $6\frac{1}{2}$ ft; 2 m.)

'Nana' is a very reliable, more compact form of bright green prickly foliage. With its completely flat dense habit, it is excellent for suppressing weeds. This distinctive cultivar is a favourite with collectors. (Ultimate spread 4 ft; 1.2 m.)

J. recurva, the drooping juniper of the Himalayas, has a graceful, botanical variety in var. *coxii*. Eventually a large tree, but slow-growing in cultivation, this has rich green foliage held tightly to the thin branchlets and a delightful weeping habit.

'Densa'* has smaller foliage than var. *coxii* and is low-growing and compact. The spreading semi-prostrate branches nod gently at the tips and it will do best in full sun. ($1\frac{1}{4} \times 2$ ft; 40–60 cm.)

J. rigida, the needle juniper, is very prickly indeed and normally a tallish shrub with drooping tips. However, 'Prostrata'* is, as the name suggests, a low-growing plant of dense habit with yellowish brown branchlets.

J. sabina, the savin juniper, and its forms are mainly low-growing shrubs of spreading habit. 'Tamariscifolia' is by far the best and quickly makes a mat of dark green foliage, which is useful for covering unsightly areas (1×4 ft; 30×120 cm.)

J. scopulorum, a species from the mountains of western North America, has given rise to many named forms, the majority of them narrow pyramids of silver-grey. 'Repens' is one of the prostrate forms, with long brown stems and bluish green foliage. It is slow-growing and spreads to 4 feet (1.2 m).

J. squamata has produced two selections of an outstanding blue. They provide a striking contrast when planted among green and gold conifers.

'Blue Carpet', a semi-prostrate form of intense blue, is thickly furnished with prickly foliage and will spread to about 5 feet (1.5 m). Any rising branches should be removed when they appear to keep it low.

'Blue Star' is one of the best dwarf conifers and therefore relatively easy to obtain. A sturdy little plant of irregular outline, it makes a compact bush. ($1\frac{1}{4} \times 1\frac{1}{2}$ ft; 40×50 cm; see opposite.)

'Glassell'*, with short grey-green leaves similar to those of *J. recurva*, is very slow-growing. The near vertical branches have

The very slow-growing *Juniperus squamata* 'Blue Star' remains dense and low

short side branchlets which curve gently downwards, forming an attractive dense little bush.

'Loderi', a well-known cultivar, is a low column of blue-green colour. The short needles are densely arranged on upright branches. ($3\frac{1}{4}$–5 ft; 1–1.5 m.)

'Pygmaea'* is one of the smallest forms of the species, with grey-green leaves. A stocky little plant, it is very similar to 'Glassell' but without the curving branchlets. ($3\frac{1}{4} \times 3\frac{1}{4}$ ft; 1 × 1 m.)

J. virginiana, another North American species, is represented by many named forms, most of which grow too tall for inclusion here. There are a few exceptions.

'Blue Cloud' is compact and slow-growing with bright blue-grey foliage. Although very dense in the centre, it has long slightly twisted branches which give it a distinctive appearance. ($1\frac{1}{2} \times 5$ ft; 50 × 150 cm.)

'Globosa'* is a rich green, globose, compact bun, rather irregular in shape when young, becoming more symmetrical later. ($2\frac{1}{2} \times 2\frac{1}{2}$ ft; 80 × 80 cm.)

'Pendula Nana'* is a collector's item and much sought after, but difficult to obtain owing to its singularly slow growth. The long, thin, greyish green branches grow horizontally unless encouraged to form a main stem to about 1 foot (30 cm) and then allowed to droop. It needs protection from winter weather.

Larix

The larches are unusual among conifers in that they shed their leaves for the winter. Most people will be familiar with the striking golden yellow colour of *Larix decidua* in a woodland in autumn. In spring too the trees look most attractive as the buds burst open to reveal fresh, bright green, new leaves.

L. decidua, the European larch, has a particularly fine dwarf form called 'Corley'* which, although not readily available, is certainly worth seeking out. It forms a low rounded bush of slow growth. ($2 \times 3\frac{1}{4}$ ft; 60 × 100 cm.)

L. kaempferi, the Japanese larch, is a beautiful species with red-brown bark and twigs. There are two dwarf forms of note.

'Nana'* is typical of a witch's broom with its dense compact habit and makes a very dwarf globose bush. ($1\frac{1}{2}$ ft; 50 cm.)

'Varley'* has a slower annual growth rate, but its longer leaves give it a very dense habit.

Picea

In their natural state the spruces are highly ornamental trees, generally of narrow pyramidal outline, and of course much too large for most gardens. They thrive in moist but well-drained soil and in long spells of dry weather they benefit from being sprayed with water, which helps to prevent attacks by mites and subsequent loss of the leaves.

P. abies, the well-known Norway spruce, is much used in forestry and especially for the production of Christmas trees. The numerous dwarf and slow-growing forms of this species are popular for rock gardens or as specimen plants, ranging from the tall strong varieties to the low-growing and very dwarf.

'Clanbrassiliana' eventually becomes a small conical bush. With its short rigid branches, it is dense and compact and has a very slow rate of growth. ($3\frac{1}{4}$ ft; 1 m.)

Above: Foliage of *Larix*, left, and *Picea*, right
Below: 'Gregoryana', one of the best dwarf forms of *Picea abies*, was
introduced in the 1850s (see p. 112)

'Elegans' was one of the earliest forms to be named. Short branches and small leaves make this an extremely compact plant and the reddish brown buds contrast pleasantly with the light green leaves.

'Gregoryana' is a most distinctive cultivar with its prickly leaves of light green. A low dense cushion, it becomes more irregular in outline with age. (6 × 8 in.; 15 × 20 cm; see p. 111.)

'Little Gem' is a diminutive plant, forming a tight little bun with very small leaves and branches.

'Nidiformis' has been well known for many years. Its spreading branches make a flat-topped plant of uniform shape. ($1\frac{1}{4}$ × 2 ft; 40 × 60 cm.)

'Procumbens' is low and spreading, with branches held in layers and tips rising slightly. (1 × $6\frac{1}{2}$ ft; 30 × 200 cm; see opposite.)

'Pygmaea', an old favourite and very slow-growing, is a compact conical bush. It tends to produce branches of normal growth which vary in vigour and must be removed. ($1\frac{1}{2}$ ft; 50 cm.)

P. glauca, the white spruce of Canada, has foliage of dark glaucous green and has given us the most consistently popular dwarf form in 'Albertiana Conica'. This is a first-class garden plant of conical shape and neat compact habit. ($2\frac{1}{2}$ ft; 80 cm.)

'Alberta Globe' is a branch sport of 'Albertiana Conica', recently introduced, and forms a low neat mound. It is much in demand as a rock garden plant. ($1\frac{1}{2}$ ft; 50 cm.)

'Laurin'* is identical to 'Albertiana Conica', but smaller in all its parts. (10 in.; 25 cm.)

P. mariana has given rise to the attractive blue-grey 'Nana', which is the most popular dwarf form of this species. It is a neat little rounded bush with branches regularly arranged from the centre. ($1\frac{1}{2}$ × $3\frac{1}{4}$ ft; 50 × 100 cm.)

P. omorika, the Serbian spruce, is a graceful slender tree and, in its native habitat on limestone slopes in Yugoslavia, it is an impressive sight. The bicoloured leaves of green above and greyish blue below are a pleasing attribute.

'Nana' is an excellent dwarf form in which the foliage colour combination is very noticeable. Eventually pyramidal in shape, this lovely compact plant will reach 4 feet (1.2 m.)

P. × mariorika, is a hybrid of P. mariana and P. omorika, which occurred in a European nursery and is intermediate between its parents. There are a few good dwarf selections.

Above: *Picea abies* 'Procumbens', a distinctive flat-topped plant with stiff, widespreading sprays of foliage
Below: 'Globosa', a superb dwarf form of the Colorado spruce, *Picea pungens* (see p. 114)

'Gnom', sometimes offered as *P. omorika* 'Gnom', is a dense conical plant with very sharply pointed needles, green above and whitish beneath. (2¼ ft; 75 cm.)

'Kobold' is a more globose shape and the needles are dark green on the underside and whitish above. (2½ × 5 ft; 75 × 150 cm.)

'Machala' has foliage which is bluish green and silvery and makes a wide-spreading, flatly globose plant. (About 1½ × 3¼ ft; 50 × 100 cm.)

P. orientalis, a tall handsome tree from the Caucasus mountains, is a neat densely branched pyramid with dark green needles which are shorter than those of *P. abies*. There are a few cultivars, most of which ultimately become quite tall.

'Gracilis', a slow-growing form with typically dense habit, starts as a round-topped bush. However, the new growth rises to produce a network of branches pointing in all directions and once a dominant leader has emerged, it becomes a more pyramidal small tree. (4 ft; 1.2 m.)

'Nana'* is a smaller version of 'Gracilis' and quite rare in cultivation. It has very dark green needles and is a globose to oval plant, usually not more than 3¼ feet (1 m) high.

P. pungens, the Colorado spruce, has an exceptional range of forms with intense blue foliage. Many of the named cultivars, although slow-growing, eventually develop into large shrubs and are ideal specimens or spot plants for the lawn.

'Globosa' is a true dwarf, whose silvery blue leaves are smaller than normal. The closely arranged branches form a thick bushy plant which is excellent for the smaller garden. (2 × 2 ft; 60 × 60 cm; see p. 113.)

'Glauca Prostrata' and other procumbent varieties are usually the result of propagating from side branches and, because these shoots are weaker, they prefer to hug the ground. This slow-growing, semi-prostrate cultivar gives a striking display of bright blue foliage, particularly when draping a wall or bank with its irregular growth.

Pinus

The pines are probably the most easily recognized group of conifers and include many large attractive trees, as well as others from mountainous regions suitable for small gardens. The numerous different species cover a wide geographical area, distributed throughout the northern hemisphere from the Arctic Circle down to the Equator. Pines are well suited to poor drier

Foliage of *Pinus*: 2 leaves, left; 3 leaves, right; 5 leaves, centre

conditions and are less demanding than other conifers. The narrow needles are held in either twos, threes or fives, according to species, and vary in length. The genus is represented by many ornamental forms of great garden value.

P. aristata is a natural slow grower, owing to the influence of the dry mountain conditions of its native home of southwestern North America, and some specimens in the wild are believed to be the oldest living trees on earth. It has great character and grows into an attractive upright bush, thickly covered with grey-blue needles which are more bunched at the tips—whence the common names bristlecone and foxtail pine. It is easily distinguished by the droplets of resin on the needle tips. ($3\frac{1}{4}$ ft; 1 m.)

P. cembra, the Arolla pine from the mountains of central Europe and northern Asia, is a highly ornamental species of neat regular outline and broadly conical habit. The short bluish green needles are held in groups of five and densely clothe the stems. (Eventually $6\frac{1}{2}$ ft; 2 m.)

'Aureovariegata'* has yellowish needles, the colour being at its best in winter, and is slower growing.

(Some nurseries may offer cultivars with the names 'Globe' and 'Pygmaea', but these have now been assigned to *P. pumila*. See p. 120).

P. contorta, the lodgepole pine, is a relatively small species from North America and varies according to its location from a contorted shrub to a tall columnar tree. One particularly good dwarf form which should become popular is 'Spaan's Dwarf'*, an open low bush with pairs of short mid-green needles closely set on the upright branches. ($2\frac{1}{2}$ ft; 75 cm.)

P. densiflora is much used in its native Japan for landscape planting, because of its irregular growth pattern and adaptability to pruning. There are a number of named cultivars, a few of which make good dwarf trees.

'Alice Verkade' is an attractive dome-shaped plant with typically long bright green needles held in pairs. ($3\frac{1}{4}$ ft; 1 m.)

'Globosa' is a low and rounded plant, with shorter needles than usual and a very dense habit. (See p. 118.)

'Umbraculifera', which means 'umbrella-like', is an apt name for this slow-growing form with upright and spreading branches and dense dark green needles. ($3\frac{1}{4} \times 3\frac{1}{4}$ ft; 1×1 m.)

P. leucodermis, a strong-growing species from the Balkan

mountains, has characteristically dense and rigid dark green needles. It is sometimes to be found under the name *P. heldreichii* var. *leucodermis*.

'Compact Gem' makes a lovely specimen plant. Initially a low rounded bush, it becomes more pyramidal as the main stems increase in height. (4 × 3 ft; 120 × 90 cm.)

'Schmidtii'* may be offered under the name 'Pygmy' but is very rare. It becomes a tight small dome of dark green rigid foliage and is ideal for growing in a pot. (See p. 118.)

P. mugo, the mountain pine, is a very variable species in the wild and ranges from a low dwarf to a small shrubby tree. Unnamed plants in a nursery may turn out to be more vigorous than they seem and it is wise to bear this in mind when deciding on their position in the garden. There are a number of excellent named forms and most are easily obtainable.

'Corley's Mat'* is reliably prostrate, forming a mat of dark green leaves not more than 1 foot (30 cm) high and about 3 feet (90 cm) spread. (See p. 119.)

'Gnom', from Holland, is probably one of the best known selections. It is a compact little bush of 2½ feet (80 cm).

'Mops' is very similar, but a little lower and wider and consequently more bun-shaped.

P. parviflora, the Japanese white pine, is a superb small species in its own right and a great favourite for bonsai in its native land. The fine blue-grey needles are held in clusters of five and it has a pleasing irregular outline and very slow growth. The species itself is well worth giving garden room and there are also several cultivars.

'Adcock's Dwarf'*, selected in Britain, is a dense bush of extremely slow growth and rather irregular outline. It has short greyish needles more clustered at the tips of the slender stems. (1½ ft; 50 cm.)

'Negishi', a Japanese name meaning short-needled, may be applied to several different selections. As a rule it makes a low, almost pyramidal, bush with irregular branching and small glaucous leaves.

'Brevifolia' is more upright and narrow in habit, with short, stiff, bluish green needles. (Eventually 4ft; 1.2 m.)

P. pumila is another Japanese pine, very similar to *P. cembra* but usually lower in habit and smaller in all its parts. It has comparatively short glaucous green leaves.

'Dwarf Blue'* is a choice plant of low, broad, bushy habit. The

Above: *Pinus densiflora* 'Globosa', a slow-growing hemispherical bush (see p. 116)
Below: The choice *Pinus leucodermis* 'Schmidtii', recorded as growing only 1½ ft (50 cm) in 40 years (see p. 117)

Above: 'Corley's Mat', a recently introduced ground-hugging form of *Pinus mugo* (see p. 117)
Below: *Pinus pumila* 'Dwarf Blue', a desirable but uncommon plant (see p. 117)

bundles of blue-grey needles with distinct white bands give it great attraction (1½ × 4 ft; 50 × 120 cm; see p. 119.)

'Globe' a globose bush of dense blue-grey colour, is becoming better known. It is very slow-growing, producing cones when quite young and red male flowers in the spring.

P. strobus, the Weymouth pine, is a large beautiful tree from North America. The long, thin, pale blue-green needles are carried in groups of five and it readily gives rise to variations from seed.

'Densa'* has shorter needles than normal, which are exceptionally thin. Still new to cultivation, it should maintain its compact, dense habit and remain low for many years.

'Nana', the most popular form, is so thickly covered with needles that the branches are completely hidden. It becomes a compact globe. (2½ × 3¼ ft; 75 × 100 cm.)

'Prostrata' needs space to develop and the procumbent branches of normal-sized foliage will in time make quite a large spreading plant.

P. sylvestris, the Scots pine, is the most familiar and recognizable conifer in the British Isles. It has a tendency to produce witch's brooms, which has led to the introduction of numerous dwarf selections from this source, in addition to many others of seedling origin.

'Beuvronensis' has been in the trade for a long time and is typical of the dense habit of a witch's broom. It makes a broad compact bush of grey-green and may require occasional pruning to maintain the density. (2½ × 3¼ ft; 75 × 100 cm.)

'Aurea' a distinct slow-growing form, has leaves of deep yellow in winter, turning to pale green in summer.

'Gold Coin' and 'Gold Medal' are two excellent coloured varieties, both light green in summer changing to an intense golden yellow in winter. They should be planted in full sun for the best display and are of upright compact habit. 'Gold Medal' will grow to about 2 feet (60 cm); 'Gold Coin' (opposite) will be taller.

'Doone Valley'*, a miniature which is perhaps the most compact of the dwarf forms, is perfect for the rock garden. It will eventually become a broad conical bush of irregular outline with blue-green needles. (1¼ × 1 ft; 40 × 30 cm.)

'Globosa' sometimes known as 'Glauca Globosa', is low-growing and compact. It makes a small globose shrub, with the short grey-green needles held on stiff upright branches.

'Globosa Viridis', despite its name, is entirely different and has a dense, almost shaggy, appearance with its long, dark green,

Above: 'Gold Coin', a reliable dwarf variety of *Pinus sylvestris* with stronger colouring than 'Aurea'
Below: *Pinus sylvestris* 'Watereri', an upright form originally found on a Surrey common in the mid-nineteenth century (see p. 122)

slightly twisted needles. It starts as low and globose, becoming more oval in time. (About 3¼ ft; 1 m.)

'Moseri' is a well-established cultivar similar to 'Globosa Viridis', distinguished from it by the fact that the long green needles turn an attractive yellow in winter.

'Nana' is a small bushy plant of very slow growth and blue-grey needles. (1½ ft; 50 cm.)

'Watereri', occasionally found under the name 'Pumila', is like 'Nana' but more vigorous. Although slow-growing, it will ultimately be quite a substantial small tree of broadly conical shape. (5 ft; 1.5 m; see p. 121.)

Pseudotsuga

P. menziesii, the Douglas fir of North America, has foliage very similar to Abies but narrower and softer. Of the few species in this genus, it is the one most commonly cultivated, both for timber and in gardens. Over the years a number of cultivars have been introduced, but only a few dwarf forms are now available from nurseries.

'Brevifolia' is an extremely slow-growing shrubby form to begin with, although eventually it becomes a small tree. The short, narrow, light green leaves are held densely around the branchlets. (2½ ft; 75 cm.)

'Densa'* is a dumpy little plant with a flat top and irregular habit, suitable for the rock garden. It has short dark green needles on twiggy, horizontally held branches. (Eventually 3¼ ft; 1 m.)

'Glauca' is a blue-leaved form and slower-growing than the species. A seedling from this named 'Fletcheri' is probably the most popular of the Douglas firs. A fine blue colour, it grows into a compact more or less rounded shrub of irregular outline and with a flat top. (2 ft; 60 cm.)

Taxus

The yews are a group of conifers of considerable garden merit. They are very hardy and tolerant of most types of soil and situation, being particularly useful in areas of heavy shade. Like the juniper, the seed of the yew is encased in a berry-like fruit which is normally red, although there is a yellow-fruited form of T. baccata.

T. baccata, the common English yew, has given us the most variation in form and colour.

'Adpressa Aurea', a gold form which is less vigorous than

Foliage of *Pseudotsuga*, left, and *Taxus*, right

'Adpressa', makes a dense spreading shrub. The small yellowish leaves are more golden in the spring when the new growth begins. (Eventually 5 ft; 1.5 m.)

'Amersfoort' is an unusual open-growing shrub, with small rounded leaves held on upright branches. ($3\frac{1}{4}$ ft; 1 m.)

'Compacta', with normal dark green foliage, is a most attractive compact, conical bush of upright branches. (Ultimately 4 ft; 1.2 m.)

'Ericoides', a small upright bush, has small glossy green leaves held closely to the stems. (Eventually 3¼ft; 1 m.)

'Nutans' is a tiny, dense, dumpy bush, with a flat top and dark green leaves on short upright branches. (1 ft; 30 cm.)

'Repandens', low-growing and spreading, is particularly valuable for ground cover in shade, and also does well. in sun. (1½–6½ ft; 50–200 cm.)

'Repens Aurea', another prostrate variety, has bright yellow variegated leaves. It will lose the variegation if grown in shade.

'Standishii', a very well known cultivar, is extremely slow-growing. It forms a small solid column of bright golden yellow. (1½ ft; 50 cm.)

'Summergold', a fairly recent introduction, has bright golden yellow foliage and is semi-prostrate. (1½ × 3¼ ft; 50 × 100 cm.)

T. cuspidata, the Japanese yew, is very hardy and is often grown in colder areas where T. baccata will not survive. There are some good dwarf forms.

'Aurescens' is a charming low compact shrub whose new golden yellow shoots turn green later in the season. (1 × 3 ft; 30–90 cm.)

'Densa' is a broad and low plant of dense dark green leaves on short branches. (1½ ft; 50 cm.)

Thuja

The arborvitae are sometimes confused with the genus *Chamaecyparis* since they bear the same type of flattened foliage sprays. The most obvious difference is the shape of the cones, which are oblong on thujas and globular on *Chamaecyparis*, while the leaves of the thujas have a distinctively pungent smell when crushed. Like *Chamaecyparis* the thujas are also prolific in the production of dwarf forms.

T. occidentalis, an American species, has a number of good dwarf forms, mostly with normal adult foliage, a few with juvenile leaves.

'Caespitosa' is a small globose bun of compact habit and flattened adult foliage. (1 × 1½ ft; 30 × 40 cm.)

'Ericoides', a fairly vigorous, juvenile-foliaged form, is a striking bronze colour in winter. (3¼ ft; 1 m.)

'Filiformis' is a very distinct cultivar and has long thread-like branches of a rich green contrasting with the orange-brown stems. (2½ ft; 80 cm.)

124

Above: Foliage of *Thuja*
Below: *Thuja occidentalis* 'Rheingold', indispensable for its golden winter colour (see p. 126)

'Globosa', a widely grown variety of compact adult foliage, forms a neat symmetrical globe of light greyish green and keeps its colour throughout the year. ($3\frac{1}{4}$ ft; 1 m.)

'Golden Globe' is an outstanding golden colour with a compact globose habit. (Ultimately 4ft; 1.2 m.)

'Little Gem' becomes a flattened mound of compact, rich green, adult foliage. It has a rather untidy habit with the branches held in a haphazard fasion. ($1\frac{1}{4}$ ft; 40 cm.)

'Rheingold' is undoubtedly one of the best known conifers in gardens. Initially a rounded bun of rich gold, it gradually gains a more pyramidal shape. It is a beautiful colour and a useful plant for any garden, although there are various forms sold under this name which grow up to 10 feet (3 m) high. ($2\frac{1}{4}$ ft; 70 cm; see p.125.)

T. *orientalis*, from China, is easily distinguished from other thujas by the foliage. This is held in vertical sprays which look as if they have been slotted together. There are several excellent and reliable dwarf forms including some with juvenile foliage.

'Aurea Nana' is commonly grown and easily obtainable. A compact oval bush of deep yellow, it needs to be grown in full sun to keep its colour and dense habit. ($3\frac{1}{4}$ ft; 1 m; see opposite.)

'Semperaurescens' is similar in habit and colour, but much more vigorous and it would soon outgrow its place in rock garden. So too would 'Elegantissima', which turns bronze in winter. Both are more appropriate for a border. (4 ft; 1.2 m.)

'Conspicua' is also a quick grower, more columnar in shape, and retains its golden colour through the winter. (See opposite.)

'Collen's Gold' and 'Golden Minaret' are two new golden introductions, both slow-growing. 'Collen's Gold' has an upright narrow habit, whereas 'Golden Minaret' forms a slender cone-shaped plant. (4 ft; 1.2 m.)

'Juniperoides', a juvenile-foliaged form, is outstanding for its plum colour in winter. In summer the soft foliage is green and it forms a dense rounded bush of about $3\frac{1}{4}$ feet (1 m).

'Rosedalis', another popular juvenile-foliaged form, is a neatly rounded and compact bush. Its particular attraction is the range of colours it assumes through the year, from the bright yellow of its spring growth to green in summer and then purplish in winter. ($3\frac{1}{4}$ ft; 1 m.)

'Sieboldii' is the green counterpart of the yellow adult foliage forms. Very densely clothed with the usual vertical branches, it forms a round-topped bush and would have a rate of growth intermediate between 'Aurea Nana' and 'Semperaurescens'.

T. *plicata*, the western red cedar, comes from the forests of

Above: Conifer garden, *Thuja orientalis* 'Aurea Nana' (on left) with other
dwarf and slow-growing varieties and heather underplanting
Below: Among the golden forms of *Thuja orientalis*, 'Conspicua' is valuable
for keeping its colour throughout the year

western North America. It is a large stately tree, important for the production of high-quality timber for the building trade. The aromatic foliage is similar to that of *Thuja occidentalis*. There are a few excellent dwarf forms, most of which are golden-leaved.

'Cuprea', a very slow-growing dwarf conical bush, is unlikely to exceed $2\frac{1}{2}$ to $3\frac{1}{4}$ feet (75–100 cm). The compact bronze-yellow foliage sprays spread slightly at the tips.

'Rogersii' is similar in colouring, but makes a globose bush with denser foliage, green on the less exposed parts of the plant and golden bronze on the outside. It is probably the best known cultivar. (Ultimately $3\frac{1}{4}$ ft; 1 m; see opposite.)

'Stoneham Gold' also has a similar colour combination, the inner foliage being very dark green and the tips an attractive orange-yellow. It is very slow-growing, but in time will be taller than 'Cuprea' and 'Rogersii'.

'Hillieri', a familiar all-green cultivar, is a very dense rounded shrub. It tends to produce long thin shoots, which should be removed. ($3\frac{1}{4} \times 3\frac{1}{4}$ ft; 1×1 m.)

Tsuga

The hemlocks are a major feature of the landscape of North America. The foliage is like that of the yew with its flat blunt-ended needles, except that these are much finer and thinner.

T. canadensis, alone of the species, has given us a plethora of named forms, originating mainly from North America. Among them are some very fine dwarf cultivars.

'Cole' an extremely popular prostrate variety, was found in the wild. The branches press themselves tightly to the ground, the main ones becoming characteristically bare of leaves at the centre. However, it is possible to train the leading stem upwards for a few inches to encourage a weeping habit. ($3\frac{1}{4}$ ft; 1 m.)

'Jeddeloh', a recent introduction from Europe, has semi-prostrate branches forming a flat-topped globose bush with a slightly depressed centre of light green foliage. ($1\frac{1}{4} \times 3\frac{1}{4}$ ft; 50×100 cm; see p. 130.)

'Jervis' is a true dwarf of exceptionally slow growth, with tightly compressed small foliage. The dense compacted branches give it an irregular chunky outline. (1 ft; 30 cm.)

Thuja plicata 'Rogersii' produces strong vertical shoots which may be cut out to maintain a more compact shape

Above: Foliage of *Tsuga*
Below: *Tsuga canadensis* 'Jeddeloh' originated as a selected seedling in a
West German nursery (see p. 129)

Above: 'Pendula', a spectacular weeping form of *Tsuga canadensis* (see
p. 132)
Below: Conifers are a great feature in the Valley Gardens at Windsor Great
Park

'Minima', contrary to its name, is low spreading and far from being the smallest form of the species. It is very attractive, with the branches rising at a low angle and gracefully drooping at the tips. Another cultivar named 'Bennett' is considered by some authorities to be synonymous. ($1 \times 2\frac{1}{2}$ ft; 30×75 cm.)

'Minuta'* is probably the dwarfest form in cultivation and certainly a plant to seek out. It is a diminutive bush of tightly congested branches and tiny leaves. (8 in.; 20 cm.)

'Pendula' is a slow-growing form that needs initial training of the main stem to the desired height for the weeping habit to be fully appreciated. If left to its own devices, it will become procumbent and spreading rather than pendulous. (See p. 131.)

Such a vast number of conifer cultivars have appeared in cultivation over a long period that it is impossible to do justice to them all and these descriptions can only scratch the surface. Although most good nurseries and garden centres offer the popular forms, it is the specialist nurseries that stock the rare and the unusual. They are well worth visiting to see the exciting range available.

Opposite: *Picea pungens*, the Colorado spruce, has many blue-grey-foliaged cultivars known collectively as the Glauca group
Below: The popular dwarf, *Chamaecyparis lawsoniana* 'Pygmaea Argenta', may be damaged in winter, but recovers in the next growing season

The Winter Garden

ROBERT PEARSON

Erica carnea 'Springwood Pink', touched by frost, brings colour to the garden in winter

'Lane', one of the best yellow-foliaged forms of the Lawson cypress, *Chamaecyparis lawsoniana*

Introduction

One of the most encouraging trends of recent times has been the greatly increased interest in the winter garden. One can sense a feeling in the air that this season has more to offer, much more, than had previously been realized, and its enjoyment, for weather reasons alone, is of a different kind to that experienced during the rest of the year.

With the notable exception of large plantings of highly colourful, winter-flowering heathers, especially when associated with conifers of contrasting shapes, colours and sizes, the winter garden should not be expected to provide the kind of mass spectacles so easy to arrange in most gardens of reasonable size at other seasons. The pleasures of the winter garden tend to be more individualistic, but none the less beguiling.

In winter one takes in the detail of flower, leaf and berry with enhanced perception, and thrills to the artistry of nature in countless ways. It might be the air of mystery of a group of trees and shrubs in the early morning mist, or the beautiful patterns and colourings of tree barks – some shrub barks too – when they are lit by low midday sun. It could be the set of a tree's branches, leafless and thrown into sharp relief, or the perfect form of some conifer.

An indispensable winter-flowering evergreen is the laurustinus, *Viburnum tinus*, which has been in British gardens for three centuries. Mahonia hybrids such as *Mahonia × media* 'Charity' and 'Lionel Fortescue', with the bonus of magnificent foliage, are other evergreens which whet the appetite. And so one could go on, and on.

Of course, we are lucky in these islands. Not only have we got, arguably, the finest climate in the world for adventurous gardening, but we are heirs to a garden flora of almost unimaginable richness. This Aladdin's cave of treasures includes much of relevance to winter, as I show in the pages which follow. Trees, shrubs, conifers, herbaceous perennial and bulbous plants are all represented here. So let us move on to the detail, allowing that in a book of this length I have had to be selective in my choice of plants. Also, I would emphasize that the plant dimensions I have given are intended as a guide only, for these can vary according to the growing conditions. So can flowering times, depending on the weather, by as much as several weeks – witness the very mild winters at the end of the 1980s.

Creating Winter Effects

If we all had the artistry of the best garden designers, how wonderful it would be. Of course, we haven't, but I am constantly amazed at the achievements of so many gardeners faced with garden-making challenges. Enthusiasm and a degree of imaginative insight, allied to a good working knowledge of plants, are the qualities most needed to achieve success, plus large doses of realism. The learning process for all of us never ceases.

When choosing plants for the garden and finding them homes, there is a need – even a duty – to give prime consideration to their cultural requirements. This might sound blindingly obvious, but it is remarkably easy to get so carried away that plants are put where you would most like to see them, and to just hope that all will be well. Sometimes it might be, but more often it won't.

I'm not thinking of anything as extreme as attempting to grow lime-hating plants in alkaline soils, or even subjecting plants which demand sharp drainage to soils which retain more than average amounts of moisture. It is more a question of committing such solecisms as putting plants which need shade in fully sunny positions (or vice versa), or those which are sensitive to cold winds in exposed places. Another common mistake is not allowing plants – trees, shrubs and conifers especially – room in which to develop properly. It is sometimes difficult to imagine that the small plant sitting in its container at your feet waiting to be planted may one day be a matronly-looking shrub of considerable size or a tree with its topmost branches 40 ft (12 m) off the ground.

That said, however, it is obviously advisable to have as many winter-decorative plants as possible in positions where they can be enjoyed to maximum advantage, which means, in practice, focusing attention on parts of the garden adjacent to the home. Key positions, too, must be those areas of the garden which are within line of sight from inside the house. Such vistas taking in plants of special significance can give enormous pleasure.

It was with thoughts like this in mind that I planted a couple of specimens of *Cotoneaster* 'Cornubia' at the bottom of my drive near the house, to provide rich autumnal and winter colour with their berries. In fact, although they are not left alone by the birds, these bright red berries, borne with such abundance, continue their display well into the new year. Opposite them, against the house wall facing south-east, a now-venerable specimen of the lovely *Garrya elliptica* (surely one of the finest of winter-flowering

The fast-growing *Garrya elliptica* is a magnificent evergreen shrub for a wall

shrubs) reaches to the eaves and delights in January and February with its mass of grey-green catkins. In view from the same vantage point, there is a brick wall clothed with the variegated form of the Persian ivy, *Hedera colchica* 'Dentata Variegata', and one of the best of the hollies for foliage effect, *Ilex aquifolium* 'Golden Queen'. (Don't expect me to know why this male, and therefore non-berrying holly was given the name 'Golden Queen' or why the female *I. × altaclerensis* 'Golden King' was so called; nobody seems to have the answer).

From within the house we can look out over a narrow raised terrace bed, where snowdrops reside, across a swathe of lawn to a specimen of the magnificent *Mahonia × media* 'Charity', some 12 ft (3.6 m) tall and a picture in December and January when its crown of striking foliage makes a backdrop for many terminal racemes of yellow flowers. Also within this same field of vision, the lavender-flowered *Crocus tommasinianus* carpets the ground at the foot of a group of tall conifers in February and March; and, as winter draws to a close, the lovely spring snowflake, *Leucojum vernum*, in its *carpathicum* variety (with yellow-tipped petals rather than the green of the species), comes into bloom under cherries and ornamental crabs.

These are the kind of plantings to be found in many gardens up and down the country and they are illustrative of a few of the things which can be done to enhance the interest and beauty of the garden in winter.

Of course, every garden is different. We all have to take the opportunity to grow the plants which appeal to us and which are, as I've said, well suited to the existing conditions. Perhaps the perfect example of a fine and good-natured plant, able to put up with any reasonable garden situation and aspect, is the beautiful winter jasmine, *Jasminum nudiflorum*, which makes such a magnificent decoration for a wall or fence. The pyracanthas, or fire-thorns as they are called, are splendid evergreens for the walls of houses or outbuildings, again of any aspect. Their berries make a brilliant showing in autumn, and some carry the display into winter.

Crocus tommasinianus increases itself rapidly by division and seed

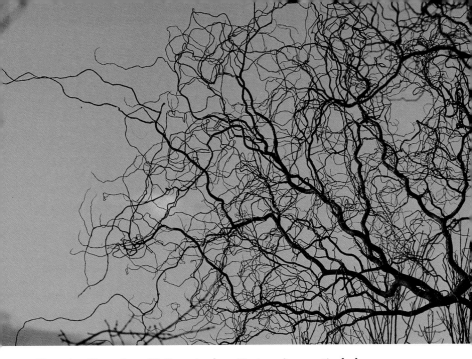

The twisted branches of *Salix matsudana* 'Tortuosa' are particularly noticeable in winter

I have already mentioned the fine evergreen foliage of the mahonias. A real tonic on any winter's day is the strong colouring of the near-indispensable *Elaeagnus pungens* 'Maculata', for its leaves cover what is a large bush with a mixture of green and golden yellow. It is always worth a prominent position.

Conifers, too, have a very special place in the winter garden for the simple reason that their shapes, colourings and foliage textures are especially prominent then. They provide a very wide range of greens, shades of yellow and blue and many different shapes from the prostrate to the bun-shaped, the cone-shaped, columnar and pyramidal. With the extremely large number of species and cultivars now available in all the leading genera, it can truly be said that there is a conifer suitable for every environment and position.

It should not be forgotten how useful a conifer screen can be to highlight the charms of winter flowers borne on bare branches, such as those of the witch hazels. The sulphur-yellow blooms of the very popular *Hamamelis* 'Pallida' have twice the impact if thrown into sharp relief in this way when lit by strong sunshine.

We are all well aware how beautiful the silhouettes of trees can be, with the tracery of bare branches and branchlets etched against a pale winter sky. Nothing quite surpasses the birches in this regard, with perhaps the elegant Swedish birch, *Betula pendula* 'Dalecarlica', my favourite. But one thinks, too, of things like the curious *Salix matsudana* 'Tortuosa', with its branches so contorted that one wonders how nature could devise such a variation from the norm; and the engaging coral bark maple, *Acer palmatum* 'Senkaki', in which the young shoots are coloured coral-red. I am sure that for most people tree silhouettes are rather low down the list of priorities when choices are being made for limited space, but I would ask you to consider this use of trees, especially when, as in the case of the birches, they have so many other virtues.

Much the same remarks apply to bark effects, which can be very beautiful. Here again the birches excel and what could be lovelier than the cherry, *Prunus serrula*, with its reddish brown, mahogany-like bark, or more exquisitely patterned than the snow gum, *Eucalyptus niphophila*? Who doesn't pause for more than a moment, too, when a bold thicket of shrubby dogwoods (*Cornus*), with their brightly coloured stems, comes into view?

For lifting the spirits sky-high, however, one has to turn to the earlier-flowering bulbs, part of whose appeal must be that winning combination of beauty and seeming vulnerability. Most, as we well know, are in physical terms quite capable of coping with our winter weather. Just think of them – the snowdrops, the winter aconites and, from February onwards, the host of crocuses, the dwarf Reticulata irises and the first of the Cyclamineus daffodils like 'February Gold'.

For obvious reasons, the number of really decorative herbaceous perennials which provide a display in winter is quite limited; but quality makes up for quantity when you recall the hellebores, especially the aristocratic-looking Corsican hellebore, *Helleborus corsicus*, as well as the delectable Algerian iris, *Iris unguicularis*, and the lovely old reddish purple-flowered *Primula* 'Wanda'.

And so we come to a pansy which, in the past few years, has taken the gardening world by storm: the F_1 Universal Strain has put an entirely different complexion on winter bedding by providing winter-long bright colour for beds and borders and for tubs, window boxes and many different kinds of container. From sowings made between May and the end of July, plants will be available for planting out in autumn, to come into flower and continue their display, in all but the worst weather conditions, until the following spring. Mixed colours are available or separate colours from purple and orange to red, shades of blue, yellow and white, some self colours, others with contrasting blotches. If you cannot raise your own plants, then garden centres offer them in

The delightful *Narcissus* 'February Gold' sometimes lives up to its name, but more often flowers in early March

the autumn, in either single or mixed colours. All in all, could you ask for more from such a splendid strain?

Perhaps our primary objective in all our garden-making (and this does not apply only to planting for winter effect) is to end up with a garden which is in harmony with itself and its surroundings. There should be no maladroit juxtaposing of plants or plant features which will strike a jarring note. One should always seek to provide interest for the eye at different levels too, which is easy enough to do using trees and shrubs with strong profiles or climbers and wall shrubs, like the ivies and the extremely handsome *Magnolia grandiflora*.

If the lawn really comes into its own between spring and autumn, that is in no way to downgrade its importance in winter. A lawn in good condition makes a marvellous foil for garden plants at all times of year, and its greenness in winter is especially to be valued.

—— Trees and Larger Conifers ——

TREES

A small tree which could be said to personify the spirit of the winter garden is the so-called autumn cherry, *Prunus subhirtella* 'Autumnalis', which puts on its main flush of flowering from November and continues the display in milder weather right through to late March. The semi-double white flowers, pink at the bud stage, are a delight, and for those who prefer something a little different, there is a pale pink-flowered form named 'Autumnalis Rosea'. So why should it be called the autumn cherry? It would seem that, in its native Japan, it does flower in the autumn for climatic reasons. To get the most from it in terms of winter display, it should be placed in a position protected from cold winds.

The Fuji cherry, *Prunus incisa*, makes a large bushy shrub or small tree, perhaps 15 ft tall and 18 ft wide (4.5 by 5.5 m), and opens its white flowers, which are pink at the bud stage, just as spring arrives. However, it has a form, 'Praecox', which is in bloom from late January or early February. This was raised by Hillier Nurseries of Ampfield, near Romsey, Hampshire, and so far as I am aware they are still the only suppliers.

The same nursery and many garden centres now offer the outstanding hybrid, *Prunus* 'Kursar', raised by that great authority on flowering cherries, the late Captain Collingwood Ingram (from a cross, it is thought, between *P. nipponica* var. *kurilensis* and *P. campanulata*). It is a shapely tree of upright habit which smothers itself with small pink flowers of a particularly intense colour in March, and I recall seeing it one mild winter in the full flush of its flowering in February. The leaves open a rich bronze in March, almost at the same time as the flowers, and assume orange shades in autumn.

A cherry grown not for its flowers, which have little decorative value, but for its beautiful bark effects is *Prunus serrula* from western China. This makes a tree some 20 ft (6 m) tall and rather less wide and its shining brown, peeling bark can be especially appreciated in winter. Its foliage is willow-like.

The ornamental cherries grow well in any fertile, well-drained soil, but they appreciate particularly a soil which is alkaline or near to neutral on the pH scale.

I referred earlier to the attractions of the Swedish birch, *Betula*

Prunus subhirtella 'Autumnalis' can grow up to 25 ft (7.6 m) high and as wide

pendula 'Dalecarlica', in its leafless winter guise. But it is grown as much or more for the beauty of the leaves, which are narrow, deeply cut and sharp-pointed, of a soft green. In 20 years or so it will become a tree some 40 ft (12 m) tall and about half that in width, but such is its light, airy appearance that it can be accommodated even in small gardens without seeming overpowering. It has the silvery trunk colouring of the species.

The cultivar of the species which is by far the best known and most widely grown is *Betula pendula* 'Youngii', or Young's weeping birch as it is called. And very lovely it is too, with its silvery bark and its domed, mushroom-like shape formed by the mass of branches and branchlets sweeping almost to the ground. It is an ideal lawn specimen or candidate for a position on a paved patio area of reasonable size, growing some 20 to 25 ft (6–7.6 m) tall in the course of time.

One of the finest of all birches for bark effect is *Betula utilis* var. *jacquemontii* from the western Himalayas, for in this case the colouring is almost startling in its whiteness. It also has good yellow autumnal leaf colouring. It will eventually make a larger tree than the Swedish birch, but graceful like all the birches.

Come to that, could anything be more graceful than the

Betula jacquemontii, as it used to be known, is now considered a variety of the Himalayan birch, *B. utilis*

common silver birch, *Betula pendula* itself, whose sobriquet "Lady of the Woods" really says it all? This can have its place too in less formal areas of the garden, ideally at the edge of a part of the garden left wild, with semi-rough grass cut only a few times a year. Then it looks in its natural element and, if three are planted close together to form an entity, so much the better. The attractive silvery bark and delicate tracery of branches give this tree enormous charm in the winter months.

But do remember that all birches are hungry trees which take a lot out of the soil. Other plants in the vicinity could feel the effects of this and may need additional feeding.

A small tree which in my experience never fails to attract attention is the coral bark maple, *Acer palmatum* 'Senkaki', which is also grown as a shrub. It takes its common name from the coral-red colouring of the younger wood. It has an erect habit of growth, as is usual with *palmatum* forms, and will take a long time to reach a height of 20 ft (6 m). It should be grown in fertile lime-free soil which is retentive of moisture in summer but still well drained, and given a sheltered position well away from any frost pocket.

I have always had a soft spot for the snake bark maples, of which *Acer pensylvanicum* from the eastern part of North America is a notable example, its bark assuming handsome white striations to contrast with the green. Its habit is erect and its eventual height about 20 ft (6 m). It is not, however, suitable for alkaline soils and, if you garden on such, then you should turn to the Asiatic kinds and particularly *A. grosseri* var. *hersii*, the bark of which is olive green striped with white. It will have a height much like that of *pensylvanicum* after a couple of decades. Both have good autumnal leaf colouring, yellow in the case of *pensylvanicum*, red and orange with *grosseri* var. *hersii*.

The evergreen strawberry trees, which bear white pitcher-shaped flowers and red strawberry-like fruits late in the year, belong to the great Ericaceae family. They are remarkable not only for their beauty but for being lime-tolerant in a plant family which, with a few exceptions, consists of lime-haters. Of the three species and one hybrid available it is the last-mentioned, *Arbutus × andrachnoides* (a cross between *A. unedo*, a native of the Mediterranean region and south-west Ireland, and *A. andrachne*, a native of south-east Europe), which is most suitable for garden planting. It is especially lime-tolerant and bears its flowers in November or early spring, with the dark green, toothed leaves providing a telling foil. The bark is coloured brownish red and is extremely attractive.

Growth is slow but, like the species, it will eventually make a

The moosewood, *Acer pensylvanicum*, was the first of the snakebark maples to be introduced to cultivation

low-branched tree. To ensure successful establishment, it is necessary to plant a young specimen straight from the pot in which it has been raised, either in spring or early autumn. The site should be sheltered from cold winds and not near a frost pocket.

Numerous willows have attractive bark colourings, among them the bright yellow-stemmed *Salix alba* var. *vitellina* and the orange-red-stemmed *S. alba* 'Britzensis' ('Chermesina'), the golden willow and the scarlet willow respectively. The first becomes a large and the second a sizable tree in the normal course of events, but they can both be stooled (hard pruned each spring) once they have grown main stems of several feet in height, and so be kept small and produce a supply of young, highly coloured wood. The colour intensity increases as the winter advances and makes for a very decorative feature.

I have never felt the urge to add the extraordinary form of the Peking willow, *Salix matsudana* 'Tortuosa', to my garden, but I can well understand its appeal, for the remarkable contortions of its branches and branchlets demand attention, particularly in winter. This cultivar from northern China has been dubbed the dragon's claw willow, and it is especially lovely when the new leaves open a fresh green colour in spring.

Willows, of course, love plenty of moisture at the roots, but they are suitable for growing in all soils which do not dry out excessively.

The snow gum, *Eucalyptus niphophila*, has proved to be remarkably hardy in Britain as eucalypts go; so, of course, has that much longer resident in our gardens and therefore far better-known species, *E. gunnii*, the cider gum. Both are extremely attractive in terms of foliage and bark colouring, particularly *E. niphophila*. Even so, they should not be expected to cope with the conditions prevailing in very cold, exposed gardens.

The snow gum in its natural habitat grows at heights of up to 6,500 ft (2,000 m) in the mountains straddling the states of New South Wales and Victoria in Australia. The patterns which form on its bark as it matures are like beautiful abstract paintings in soft shades of green, grey and cream, while the branchlets are coloured red in winter before assuming a bluish white bloom in

The scarlet willow, *Salix alba* 'Britzensis', is more of a shrub when hard pruned for winter effect

spring. The leaves are large, grey green and glossy. All in all it is a dream of a small tree which can reach a height of 20 ft (6 m) in ten years.

Eucalyptus gunnii is much faster growing and makes a tree at least 40 ft (12 m) in height, with juvenile, rounded foliage of bright silvery blue and adult foliage of lanceolate shape and a distinctive jade green. Flower arrangers like to stool their plants each spring to get a regular supply of juvenile foliage.

Eucalypts are best planted in late spring or early June, when there is no more chance of frost occurring, straight from the pots in which they have been raised. A sunny, sheltered position should be chosen where the soil is not lacking in moisture. In particular, make sure that the soil does not dry out in the months following planting. They are not suitable for growing on thin, chalky soils.

The Cornelian cherry, *Cornus mas*, is sometimes seen as a small tree, perhaps 20 to 25 ft (6–7.6 m) tall, and at other times as a large shrub. It bears clusters of yellow flowers on the bare stems in late winter and these may be followed by red, oblong fruits, from

The snow gum, *Eucalyptus niphophila*, is relatively slow-growing and hardy

Left: *Cornus mas*, a European native, has been cultivated for centuries in Britain
Right: *Malus* 'Red Sentinel', the hybrid crab, was highly rated in Dutch trials in the early 1980s

which a preserve can be made. This is an occasion when a dark background, such as might be provided by a dark green conifer screen, is a great help to throw the flowers into strong relief. Its growth is slow, which might not be a disadvantage in smaller gardens. Plant it in a sunny position in well-drained soil, which can be acid or alkaline.

The fruiting ornamental crabs, which give such a magnificent display in autumn, can in some cases continue deep into winter (mid- to late December). The popular and readily available *Malus* 'Golden Hornet', with large, egg-shaped fruits of rich yellow, is a good example, and even more so 'Red Sentinel', which can hold on to its deep red, rather round fruits until the latter part of winter. This pair make trees at least 25 ft (7.6 m) tall and wide.

My real favourites, though, are the two small-growing *Malus × robusta* forms known as 'Red Siberian' and 'Yellow Siberian', both fine trees which bear heavy crops of their cherry-like fruits, red in the first, yellow in the second, as the names suggest. The fruits hang on the trees well into winter (until some time in December in my experience), and I have a specimen of 'Yellow Siberian' quite close to my study window so it is under close observation. Both carry a profusion of white, pink-tinged flowers in spring.

Culturally, the ornamental crabs are very adaptable, doing well in any fertile, well-drained soil in sunshine or light shade, although the best fruiting will be obtained when the trees are exposed to plenty of sunshine.

The mountain ashes (members of the Aucuparia section of the genus *Sorbus*) include numerous species and hybrids with outstanding fruiting qualities, but many have finished their display by the time winter arrives. *Sorbus esserteauiana* is one of the exceptions, for its scarlet fruits colour up late, in October, and are usually around into the new year. It is an attractive tree with a somewhat pyramidal habit, growing eventually to some 40 ft tall and 25 ft wide (12 by 7.6 m).

Another reliable early-winter performer is *Sorbus hupehensis*, perhaps 25 ft tall and up to 20 ft wide (7.6 by 6 m). This is a very pretty tree with its purplish brown stems, bluish green leaflets and white, pink-suffused berries, which remain on the tree long after the leaves have gone, often until the turn of the year. Both *esserteauiana* and *hupehensis* put on a good show of autumn leaf colour, in shades of red. They also bear abundant white flowers in May and early June. They have no fads regarding cultivation, doing well in any average soil in sunshine or light shade.

Of the female (berrying) hollies, most people who have made a study of them would probably agree that *Ilex aquifolium* 'J. C. Van Thol' is one of the very best. Dark green, evergreen leaves, which are almost spineless and glossy-surfaced, make a fine backdrop for the mass of bright red berries. Eventually it can reach a height of 30 ft with a width of 15 ft (9 by 4.5 m), but after ten years it is likely to be still only some 10 ft (3 m) tall. Hollies are far from fast growing. 'Madame Briot' is another excellent cultivar of *I. aquifolium* for producing berries. These are an intense red, combined with heavily spined leaves which are strongly marked with deep yellow. A lot smaller than these is the attractive *I. aquifolium* 'Handsworth New Silver', with creamy white-margined leaves, long and heavily spined, which complement beautifully the red berries. The superb holly with yellow-variegated foliage, *I. aquifolium* 'Golden Queen', can also make a real contribution, both in its own right and as a male holly, whose presence is necessary to effect cross-pollination and get the female hollies to bear berries.

Hollies generally are undemanding, growing well in most soils and in less than perfect atmospheric conditions. However, the yellow-variegated kinds are best exposed to as much sunshine as possible to bring out their colouring fully.

The semi-evergreen, large-leaved *Cotoneaster* 'Cornubia' is a great asset to the early winter garden with its berry display. Although more often seen as a spreading shrub, it can be grown as a standard which, with the head of arching branches, reaches a height of 12 to 16 ft (3.6–4.8 m). There are other cotoneasters grown in standard form and semi-evergreen (they lose their leaves in hard weather) which should be considered – for instance, *C.*

Sorbus hupehensis is an excellent small tree for all seasons

Ilex aquifolium 'J. C. Van Thol' is a very free-fruiting holly and, like its relatives, ideal for a small garden

'Rothschildianus', with apricot-yellow berries and a height in the region of 16 ft (4.8 m); and the much smaller and extremely attractive, weeping C. 'Hybridus Pendulus', grown as a half-standard with a height of about 10 ft (3 m), which makes it an ideal tree for small gardens. It carries a profusion of red berries well into winter. In addition, there is the deciduous Himalayan species, *C. frigidus*, a round-headed tree up to 30 ft (9 m) tall with a crop of bright red berries.

All the cotoneasters are easily pleased in a cultural sense, growing well in any well drained, reasonably fertile soil in sunshine or light shade.

CONIFERS

And so to ornamental conifers, which have such an important role to play in the garden nowadays, and in winter particularly. People like the plantsman and conifer specialist, Adrian Bloom, are past-masters at using conifers effectively, and I am impressed by the way many Germans, Dutch and Swiss include them in their gardens with such style and panache, although sometimes, to our taste, perhaps a little excessively. In the past couple of decades or so there has been a great upsurge of interest in ornamental conifers of all complexions in this country, with much of the interest stimulated by, and many of the finest introductions coming from, Bloom's Bressingham Gardens and nursery.

Conifers are available now in tremendous variety to give pleasure at all times of year. In winter, for obvious reasons, they are particularly prominent in the garden scene, and their shapes and colourings, if they are disposed with skill, add much stimulation to the eye. The larger-growing ones therefore need to be chosen with special care, to make sure that they will integrate well with other features and are given the right kind of growing conditions.

Shapes, of course, draw the eye like a magnet, as do such colours as yellow and blue. This is in no way to underestimate green – surely the most important colour in the garden with its extraordinary range of hues, some of great subtlety. One calls to mind the dark green of the magnificent Serbian spruce, *Picea omorika*, and of the soaring, ultra-slim incense cedar, *Calocedrus (Libocedrus) decurrens*, the rich green of *Chamaecyparis lawsoniana* 'Green Pillar' and 'Kilmacurragh', and the grey green of *C. lawsoniana* 'Fletcheri', with its bronze overtones in winter.

So far as I am concerned, there is no more beautiful conifer for a key position in the garden than the Serbian spruce. It is the epitome of grace, with its thick covering of dark green leaves borne on branches which curve down only to lift up again at the tips, and this combined with a narrowly pyramidal shape. A fairly average height is 50 ft (15.2 m), with a width of some 15 ft (4.5 m) at its widest point, but it will still have reached only about 12 to 15 ft (3.6–4.5 m) in height after ten years, and it is a splendid lawn specimen. It can be grown on both acid and alkaline soils provided these are fertile and well drained. In nature it is found only in the limestone mountains which abut the River Drina in Yugoslavia.

The incense cedar has an equally striking appearance, narrowly columnar to a height of 50 ft (15.2 m) or more and with a width of 8 to 10 ft (2.4–3 m), but again slow growing – only 10 ft (3 m) after ten years. It is the ultimate in accent plants, either planted on its own or in a group of three in a lawn setting, but to do such a feature justice needs more space than most of us have at our disposal. Grow it in a sunny position in a moisture-retentive soil of good quality.

The Colorado spruce, *Picea pungens*, from the south-western United States, has provided us with a selection of cultivars of varying form, and none more calculated to catch the eye than the blue spruces of conical habit and, eventually, large size, 30 ft (9 m) or more, although they are unlikely to exceed 8 ft (2.4 m) in the first ten years. These associate delightfully with other conifers of

Left: *Chamaecyparis lawsoniana* 'Green Pillar' demonstrates how valuable green can be in the garden
Right: *Picea pungens* 'Koster' is one of the most popular blue spruces

different sizes, shapes and colourings and with heathers. They also make fine lawn specimens. They should be grown in good soil which does not lack moisture and in sheltered positions well protected from icy winds. Two of the best and most widely grown are 'Hoopsii' and 'Koster', with 'Hoopsii' having the edge for quality. Both have silvery blue colouring.

Still on the blue theme, I have been much impressed by *Chamaecyparis lawsoniana* 'Pembury Blue', which will grow to a height of about 10 ft (3 m) in as many years but can in time make a tree 40 to 50 ft (12–15.2 m) tall. It has an attractive conical habit and blue-grey leaf sprays which tend to deepen in colour in winter. Without question, it is one of the best conifer introductions of recent times, certainly among the blues.

A very distinctive bluish green conifer is *Chamaecyparis lawsoniana* 'Wisselii', conical in habit and with unusual upward-facing, tufty growths. It grows to a height of about 40 ft (12 m), but only a quarter of that after ten years. A splendid bluish grey accent conifer, especially favoured for planting with heathers, is the slim *Juniperus scopulorum* 'Skyrocket' – up to 20 ft (6 m) tall eventually while still very narrow.

Conifers, with heathers and variegated ivy, contribute a range of colours to the winter garden

What is good among the larger yellow-foliaged conifers? Undoubtedly *Chamaecyparis lawsoniana* 'Lane', or 'Lanei' as it used to be called. This has the merit of holding its colour well in winter, and can be a dominant feature when fully grown to a height of perhaps 50 ft (15.2 m). However, it won't be more than 10 ft (3 m) tall after a decade of growth in most gardens, so there is no need to rule it out on the score of height. Few conifers are better for terminating a vista in a largish garden. Exposure to as much sunshine as possible will bring out to the full its golden yellow colouring.

An up and coming Dutch-raised cultivar of the Lawson cypress is 'Golden Wonder', with a conical habit and bright golden yellow colouring which has much in common with 'Lane' but more density. There is now another Dutch introduction in this colour band – a sport of *C. lawsoniana* 'Fletcheri' named 'Yellow Transparent', the allusion being to the pale yellow, rather translucent colouring of the young foliage, which assumes bronze tones in winter.

Still with the Lawson cypresses, 'Green Pillar' and 'Kilmacurragh' have many uses in the garden, both narrowly columnar and the second especially so. 'Green Pillar' is bright green and 'Kilmacurragh' a deeper green but just as rich. Both grow to about 10 ft (3 m) tall in a decade, with eventual heights of 35 to 40 ft (10.6–12 m). An ordinary, well-drained soil of average fertility is suitable for them.

One of the most interesting of the newer conifers is a form of the American arbor-vitae, *Thuja occidentalis* 'Smaragd' (it originated in Denmark, hence the rather unusual name). It has bright emerald-green colouring and makes a splendid hedge with its coiffured, pyramidal appearance and height, when so used, of about 7 ft (2 m) upwards. It is also an excellent specimen plant, which will in the end top the 20 ft (6 m) mark. It is an attractive feature in the winter garden and is as good for chalk soils as those of an acid nature.

Some further suggestions may be found in the Wisley Handbook, *Trees for Small Gardens*; dwarf and slow-growing conifers are explored in the second section of this book, pp. 75–133.

Shrubs and Climbers

SHRUBS

Shrubs are the life-blood of the modern garden – available in tremendous diversity, needing little routine attention compared with many other types of plant and always a source of potential or actual interest. They exude an air of informality which is very agreeable, whether or not they are at their season (or seasons) of greatest decorative value. Those of an evergreen nature have a special significance, of course, in winter, for they are the plants which, together with conifers, give substance to the design of the garden when deciduous trees and shrubs are leafless and so much else is taking a seasonal rest.

Nowadays, most of us tend to favour mixed borders of shrubs, perennials, bulbous plants and even annuals, although borders devoted solely to shrubs or perennials still have their place. But whichever it is, planting plans need very careful thought – as much, in the case of shrubs, about the year-round spread of interest as about the way the chosen plants will integrate with each other. In all gardens there are key vantage points and, as far as possible, one should make sure that from these there is always something to catch the eye, whatever the season. Fortunately, there is no lack of suitable material to realize such aspirations in winter.

It is a good idea also to include at least a smattering of shrubs which can be cut for indoor arrangements; these, to be enjoyed at close quarters, are especially valued in winter. There are many delightful garden shrubs which double up in this way, from the evergreen *Garrya elliptica* in all its midwinter catkinned splendour to such deciduous subjects as the winter jasmine, *Jasminum nudiflorum*, the winter sweet, *Chimonanthus praecox*, and choice viburnums like the tall *Viburnum × bodnantense* 'Dawn' and 'Deben' – the last three deliciously scented. I am no flower arranger, but I do know that I have come to appreciate, as I am sure many of you have, the true beauty of plants through the artistry of those skilled in this art form. (See also the Wisley Handbook, *Flower Arranging from the Garden*.)

It might be thought that the grandest and most imposing of all winter shrubs are the *Mahonia × media* hybrids, which have resulted from crossing *M. japonica* and *M. lomariifolia* (both fine plants, and the latter especially beautiful but alas too tender for

Above: The early-flowering *Stachyurus praecox* is another lovely shrub for flower arranging
Below: *Mahonia* × *media* hybrids like the well-known 'Charity' are especially welcome for their showy flowers and superb foliage

many of us to grow in our gardens). These include 'Charity', the first to be introduced and widely available; 'Lionel Fortescue', which is now considered the pick of the bunch; 'Winter Sun'; 'Buckland'; 'Underway'; and 'Charity Sister'. All have superb evergreen foliage of dark green; each leaf consists of up to 21 large, spiny leaflets with, in 'Charity' for instance, the total length of the leaf exceeding 1½ ft (45 cm). All have equally superb terminal sprays of flowers, borne in November and December, in varying shades of yellow. The racemes, up to 20 in each head, may be upright or more spreading depending on the cultivar. Likewise, there are variations in size and habit. 'Charity' is upright growing and up to about 14 ft (4.2 m) tall. 'Lionel Fortescue' is more bushy and not much less in height, while 'Underway' is quite a lot shorter and very bushy, to refer to three which I have in my garden. 'Underway' is a very good plant – they all are – but it has been neglected by the nursery trade for some reason, and I know of only one source for it at the time of writing (Bridgemere Garden World, a real plantsman's garden centre, at Bridgemere, near Nantwich, Cheshire, which is able to supply personal shoppers only but has all the cultivars mentioned above).

Quite apart from their outstanding decorative qualities when in flower, these mahonias give good value throughout the year with their dramatic foliage. They grow well in any fertile, well-drained soil which is reasonably retentive of moisture in summer and does not lie wet in winter.

The viburnums, both deciduous and evergreen, provide unrivalled service to us gardeners around the year in their numerous manifestations. For winter effect alone we can call on such diverse plants as the low-growing *Viburnum davidii*, 2 to 3 ft tall and up to 5 ft wide (60–90 cm by 1.5 m), which is so much used nowadays as a ground-cover shrub; the medium-sized to large *V. farreri* (the former *V. fragrans*); the large *V. × bodnantense* 'Dawn', and its counterpart of East Anglian origin, 'Deben' (raised at Notcutt's nursery, Woodbridge); and the ever reliable and most decorative evergreen *V. tinus*, the laurustinus, a real veteran which has come up with splendid modern forms like 'Gwenllian' and 'Eve Price'.

Viburnum davidii has found its true métier as a ground-cover shrub of excellence, and the handsome, narrowly oval, evergreen leaves with their prominent veining, dark green colour and leathery texture making an attractive carpet throughout the year. If you plant some male specimens with the females, then there is always the chance of getting a good show of the turquoise-blue berries, which continue well into winter.

The deciduous *Viburnum farreri*, which eventually makes a

Viburnum × bodnantense 'Dawn', a vigorous, upright shrub which produces dense clusters of flowers

bush some 10 to 12 ft (3–3.6 m) tall and wide, is very space effective, for it bears its clusters of white, highly fragrant flowers, pink at the bud stage, from around the beginning of November until at least the end of February. The two *V. × bodnantense* hybrids, 'Dawn' and 'Deben', both shrubs up to 10 ft tall and 4 to 5 ft wide (3 by 1.2–1.5 m), are a picture when the bare branches are studded with the clusters of strongly fragrant flowers. In 'Dawn', these are pink and remarkably resistant to frost damage, appearing from early December to late February usually, although the season can be some weeks longer. In 'Deben', the flowers are white, opening from pink buds, and in milder weather they can last from November until April.

If the flowers of the laurustinus, *Viburnum tinus*, lack scent, they certainly make up for it in the length of the flowering period – November to April, with only severe weather temporarily halting the display. A popular cultivar is the compact-growing 'Eve Price', a bush some 8 ft (2.4 m) tall which has white flowers with a hint of pink in them opening from carmine buds. As in the other cultivars, the dark green, oval, evergreen leaves with their glossy surfaces are a pleasing foil. The one I like best of all, however, is 'Gwenllian', in which pale pink flowers open from pink buds and, uncharacteristically, are often accompanied by small blue berries – a delightful sight intermingled with the blooms. This too grows

162

about 8 ft (2.4 m) tall and much the same in width. There is also a new white-flowered cultivar named 'Israel', which we shall probably hear more of in future.

All these viburnums can be grown in ordinary, well-drained soils which are retentive of plenty of moisture. Positions open to sunshine are best, although *V. tinus* is tolerant of shade.

Seen at its best, the evergreen *Viburnum rhytidophyllum* is a magnificent tall foliage shrub for growing in semi-shade against a wall, where it will be protected from wind, which soon damages the leaves. These are up to 7 in. (18 cm) long, oval, dark green, shiny and wrinkled, and are carried on a plant which can reach a height of 15 to 20 ft (4.5–6 m). The yellowish white flowers, borne in trusses and opening in May and June, are a very secondary feature. The fruits which follow are at first red, then black. This needs a good-quality soil, acid or alkaline, to thrive.

The daphnes include several winter-flowering shrubs with memorable fragrance, one of the most frequently grown being, of

As well as richly coloured blossom early in the year, *Daphne mezereum* bears attractive red berries in autumn

course, the mezereon, *Daphne mezereum*. This deciduous species produces purplish red flowers in February and March, clustered thickly up the stems on a plant 3 to 4 ft (90 cm–1.2 m) tall and wide. It does well on alkaline or acid soils, and its only fault is that it is sometimes liable to die without warning, owing, it is thought, to a virus infection.

Daphne odora 'Aureo-marginata' (it is best to grow this form rather than the somewhat tender species) bears dense heads of highly fragrant, white, pink-tinged flowers, reddish purple on the outside, in late winter and early spring, these framed by handsome, lanceolate, evergreen leaves which are margined with creamy white. Find it a sheltered spot where the soil is fertile and well drained but not liable to dry out in summer. Eventually, it may reach a height of as much as 6 ft (1.8m) but only after many years.

Still available only in restricted quantities, *Daphne bholua* 'Gurkha', which is deciduous, and 'Jacqueline Postill', which is evergreen, are wonderfully fragrant forms of this Himalayan daphne. The first was discovered by Major Spring Smythe in Nepal in 1962 at 10,000 ft (3,000 m), and the second is a seedling from it raised by Mr Alan Postill and named for his wife. 'Gurkha' carries purplish rose flowers between December and February on a bush up to 7 ft (2 m) tall, and the similarly sized 'Jacqueline Postill' has reddish mauve flowers, white on the inside, over a rather longer period into March. Both were introduced to the gardening public by Hillier and can now be obtained from a few other suppliers. Again, they require a good soil, acid or alkaline, well drained but retentive of moisture, and a position sheltered from cold wind.

The spurge laurel, *Daphne laureola*, a native of Europe, including Britain, and western Asia, is a very different proposition: a low-growing evergreen, 2 to 4 ft tall and up to 4 ft wide (60 cm–1.2 m by 1.2 m), it bears a wealth of glossy, lanceolate, leathery leaves among which nestle yellowish green flowers, scented but insignificant looking. It does well even in dense shade and is worth growing for its foliage effect. So is *Sarcococca humilis*, another evergreen for shade, which is 1½ ft tall and some 2½ ft wide (45 by 76 cm) and increases by suckers. The shiny, dark green leaves are narrowly oval and pointed, and fragrant white flowers are carried in tufty racemes in late winter. This and other sarcococcas are often known as Christmas box. Both they and the spurge laurel do well on alkaline soils.

Other shade-loving evergreens for winter effect which must not be overlooked are the skimmias, most of all perhaps in the shape of the hybrid *Skimmia × foremanii*. The mid-green leaves tend

Above: *Daphne odora* 'Aureo-marginata' starts flowering in late winter and continues until spring
Below: The bronzy red buds of *Skimmia japonica* 'Rubella' are decorative well before the flowers actually open

'Crotonifolia' and other forms of *Aucuba japonica* will succeed even in the shade of trees

towards the elliptic in shape and form a splendid backdrop for the mass of red berries, which last through the winter, and for the fragrant white flowers in April and May. It is a female form which needs pollinating by a male skimmia to produce berries, and what better than *S. japonica* 'Rubella'? This bears large panicles of red buds the winter through, which open to highly perfumed, white flowers in early spring. It is a slightly smaller plant than *S. × foremanii* – 3 to 4 ft (90 cm–1.2 m) tall and wide against the other's 4 to 5 ft by 6 ft (1.2–1.5 by 1.8 m). Both are suitable for alkaline soils, or any soil which is fertile and well drained, and they provide good ground cover.

In a different category, but a fine evergreen for shade, is the aucuba, *Aucuba japonica*, in its various forms. It has an affinity with the skimmias in that the sexes occur on separate plants, so that to obtain berries on the female forms a male form must be in the vicinity to effect pollination. The berries are borne in autumn and often persist long into winter. Of the female forms a good choice would be 'Crotonifolia', in which the large leaves are speckled with golden yellow and the bright red berries are freely produced. A fine male form is 'Picturata', which also has leaves marked with golden yellow. Both make bushes some 6 to 8 ft (1.8–2.4 m) tall and wide, and will do well in any average soil. The aucubas were great favourites with the Victorians and it is about time they were taken more notice of again.

Fatsia japonica and × *Fatshedera lizei* (the bigeneric hybrid which resulted from crossing *Fatsia japonica* with the Irish ivy, *Hedera helix* 'Hibernica') are dual role home-cum-garden plants of real value. These evergreen shrubs can be extremely useful for growing in shady places, although the fatshedera will do equally well in sun, and in time, they become sizeable bushes. Their handsome, shiny leaves are large, palmate and of leathery texture, up to 15 in. (38 cm) or even more across in the case of fatsia, 10 in. (25 cm) in the case of fatshedera. Both carry terminal panicles of flowers in October and November, although the green flowers of fatshedera rarely mature out of doors. The globular umbels of white flowers of the fatsia, on the other hand, are a real decorative feature and are followed by black fruits. They should be grown in sheltered positions in good soil.

Any deciduous shrub which produces its flowers in March, or as early as February given half a chance by the weather, and combines with that a winsome charm is worth our attention. Such a shrub is *Stachyurus praecox* (*praecox*, of course, meaning very early), and it surprises me that it has not been given greater attention by gardeners, for it does well in any average soil in sunshine

Corylus avellana 'Contorta' was originally discovered in a hedgerow in Gloucestershire in the 1860s

The lovely *Hamamelis* 'Pallida' was first raised in the Royal Horticultural Society's Garden at Wisley

or light shade. Pendant racemes of pale yellow, bell-shaped flowers, each about 3 in. (7.5 cm) long and including up to 20 blooms, are strung out along the bare branches of a bush some 8 to 9 ft tall and 5 ft wide (2.4–2.7 by 1.5 m).

That leads me on, calendar-wise, to another cheery sight in February, when the hazel or cob nut, *Corylus avellana*, bears its showy yellow male catkins. The species itself is a large bush, but its curious cultivar, 'Contorta', which always creates interest, is no more than 8 ft (2.4 m) tall and wide. The extraordinary shapes of the branches earned it the common name, earlier this century, of Harry Lauder's walking stick, and it is also called cockscrew hazel – more meaningful to those who know nothing of the famous Scottish comedian. In this form, too, the catkins are a real feature. Growth is slow, but cultivation is easy in sunshine or light shade.

The witch hazels of Chinese and Japanese origin, together with the hybrids to which they have given rise, offer rich pickings for the winter gardener, producing their flowers on the bare branches between late December and late February or early March. Neutral or acid soils are certainly best for them, but they are often grown on alkaline soils. A soil rich in humus and containing plenty of nutrients is what they really like.

The general consensus of opinion seems to be that the best of the Chinese witch hazels is *Hamamelis* 'Pallida'. I go along with that. It has soft sulphur-yellow flowers of good size with excellent fragrance and makes a bush some 8 ft (2.4 m) tall and wide. Another which has much to offer is the somewhat larger *H.* 'Brevipetala', with short-petalled flowers of deep yellow and heavily scented. A splendid *H. × intermedia* hybrid is 'Jelena', in which the yellow flowers have coppery red overtones.

The flowers of the witch hazels are intriguing, for the petals are strap shaped and numerous. They are also as tough as old boots, frosts not worrying them at all. Shrubs like these, blooming on the bare wood, benefit greatly from a darkish background to set off the flowers when lit by the sun. It should not be forgotten that the witch hazels have excellent autumnal colour, usually yellow but shades of red and orange in 'Jelena'.

One of the success stories of the second half of this century has been the progressive building up of a range of *Camellia × williamsii* hybrids (crosses between *C. saluenensis* and *C. japonica*). These have great garden value for anyone who can provide a lime-free soil and, even for those who cannot, there is always the possibility of growing a few specimens in suitably sized containers in, of course, lime-free compost. But then you must be careful not to let the roots become frozen in the arctic spells of weather we get briefly in some winters; either take the plants under cover or wrap sacking thickly round the containers.

The × *williamsii* hybrids combine hardiness with fine flower form and good evergreen foliage, the last being an attraction around the year. They also have an advantage over the huge number of *Camellia japonica* cultivars (which are also excellent garden shrubs) in that they drop their spent flowers cleanly, whereas the others hang on to them in an unsightly way, necessitating regular picking over. While spring is the main flowering season, there are some hybrids which start to bloom in winter. Everything depends on the geographical location and the microclimate they are subjected to, with sheltered gardens in places like Cornwall being well ahead of the field. Most fall within the 6 to 10 ft (1.8–3 m) height range at maturity, but some can get much bigger in very favourable environments. The one which is exceptionally early flowering, as its name implies, is 'November Pink' (introduced at the beginning of the 1950s). Its single, rose-pink flowers have been known to open in November and certainly grace the second half of winter and spring, up to May. 'St Ewe', another with single, rose-pink flowers (of 1947 vintage) is likely to

Camellia × williamsii 'Debbie' flowers over a long period from late winter into May

start flowering in February, as does the lovely, New Zealand-raised 'Debbie', with peony-form, rose-pink flowers. In many gardens, too, the very popular 'Donation' (one of the first to be introduced, in 1941), with semi-double, clear pink flowers, will be in flower in March. (See also the Wisley Handbook, *Camellias*.)

If you have an acid soil, there is every reason to consider growing one or two of the early-flowering (March-April) rhododendrons of modest size – say Seta or 'Tessa Roza', 4 and 5 ft (1.2 and 1.5 m) tall respectively, and with flowers, in the first case, of pale pink with deeper pink striping and, in the second, of a rosy pink hue. A group of three of one kind can be very effective. (For further information, see the Wisley Handbook, *Rhododendrons*.)

Evergreen foliage shrubs of real substance include the ubiquitous and always extremely attractive *Elaeagnus pungens* 'Maculata' which, given time, makes a solid bush 10 ft (3 m) tall and wide, and two slower-growing and smaller cultivars, 'Dicksonii' and 'Frederici'. In 'Maculata', the leaves are large and heavily marked with rich yellow; in 'Dicksonii', they are margined with yellow; and in 'Frederici', the colouring is reversed, with most of the rather narrow leaves coloured cream and a dark green margin. This last is a bush half the size of 'Maculata'. They respond to good treatment and should always be given a fertile soil to grow in, avoiding thin, chalky soils.

Elaeagnus × *ebbingei* 'Gilt Edge' is another highly decorative foliage shrub, in which the prominent evergreen leaves are broadly margined with golden yellow. This grows quite slowly to a height and spread of 6 by 5 ft (1.8 by 1.5 m). Considerably faster growing and larger is 'Limelight', which has a central blotch of yellow on its leaves. Both have leaves silvery on the undersides and can be used to good effect in the winter garden.

There are numerous easily grown cotoneasters which carry their display of red berries well into winter. Indeed, the deciduous or semi-evergreen *Cotoneaster simonsii*, 8 to 10 ft (2.4–3 m) tall and wide, will often keep its berries right through the winter. The same applies to the deciduous *C. horizontalis*, which is low growing in the open, higher against a wall, and also has prettily coloured leaves in early winter, turning red and orange and slow to fall; and to the ground-covering evergreen *C. conspicuus* 'Decorus', 2 to 3 ft (60–90 cm) tall by 6 ft (1.8 m) wide.

The mainstream forsythias might just, in calendar terms, squeeze into late winter to start their flamboyant flowering season, but such fine cultivars as *Forsythia* × *intermedia* 'Lynwood', 'Spring Glory' and 'Beatrix Farrand' are spring shrubs and I shall turn to a real winter flowerer, the Korean *F. ovata*, and its cultivar 'Tetragold'. The species makes a bush

A shapely bush of the invaluable *Elaeagnus pungens* 'Maculata'

some 5 ft (1.5 m) tall and wide, with arching branches bearing bright yellow flowers from late February or very early March. 'Tetra-gold' is a smaller version raised in Holland, with deep yellow flowers and a height and spread of about 4 ft (1.2 m). It hardly needs saying that the forsythias generally are among the easiest of deciduous shrubs to please: almost any garden soil suffices and they do well in sunshine or light shade.

No sight is more heartening on a bright winter day than the massed stems of shrubby dogwoods lit by strong sunshine and viewed perhaps across a lawn or, even better, beside some in-formal water feature. But they are pleasurable in many different situations. The pick of the bunch might well be *Cornus alba* 'Sibirica', with bright red, young stems, and *C. stolonifera* 'Flavir-amea', in which the stems are an attractive greenish yellow. They are delightful grown together.

Hard pruning annually in spring just as growth is starting ensures a supply of young, highly coloured wood, and keeps plants to a height of about 6 ft (1.8 m). They revel in damp soil, but in fact do well in any soil of reasonable quality. Always find them a home open to plenty of sunshine.

The white-stemmed ornamental bramble, *Rubus cockburni-anus*, a relative of the blackberry, is also very showy in winter. It is the first-year stems which have the attractive white bloom over-laying the purple, and the older stems should be pruned away either in autumn or early spring. It makes an open bush some 8 ft (2.4 m) tall and rather less wide, with deciduous fern-like foliage. The purplish flowers appear in early summer but are of little consequence. It is easily grown in poor soils.

Why do not more gardeners grow *Kerria japonica*, rather than its stiffer and more upright-growing, orange-yellow, double-flowered form, 'Pleniflora'? The species itself makes a lower, spreading bush 4 to 6 ft (1.2–1.8 m) tall and wide, with single, bright yellow flowers in late spring, and its vivid green stems are a joy when bare in winter. Again, it presents no problems culturally.

WALL SHRUBS AND CLIMBERS

Good use should be made of house and other tall walls to grow one or more of those evergreen pyracanthas which carry their berries over into the winter season – the excellent orange-red-berried 'Mohave', for instance, which has the additional advan-tage of being resistant to fireblight and scab, two diseases to which pyracanthas are prone; orange-red-berried 'Orange Glow'; and the well-known, red-berried 'Watereri', which is an excellent, free-standing specimen plant, usually some 8 ft tall and 10 ft wide

Above: Frosty weather gives an extra dimension to the red stems of *Cornus alba* 'Sibirica'
Below: A mixture of *Garrya elliptica* and pyracantha makes an eye-catching winter feature on a wall

(2.4 by 3 m). Another with long-persisting berries is the red-berried *Pyracantha atalantioides*, but it is probably best to steer clear of this as it is said to be susceptible to fireblight.

Similarly, a home should be found if possible for the evergreen *Garrya elliptica*, an almost indispensable component of the mid-winter garden, for there is nothing quite to compare with a full-sized specimen, possibly as much as 20 ft (6 m) tall, smothered in a grey-green waterfall of catkins during January and February. On male plants, the catkins can be as much as 12 in. (30 cm) long and certainly 9 in. (23 cm) in normal circumstances. Those of the cultivar 'James Roof' can be several inches longer still, but the species itself is rewarding enough. The smallish oval leaves are dark green and thickly borne, remaining attractive around the year. This shrub can be grown on a wall with any aspect, but do not plant it where it will be exposed to cold winds, which in extreme cases can badly brown the leaves. Provide it with a good soil. It can be grown as a free-standing shrub in many gardens, but is usually far better in a wall bed.

An evergreen wall shrub of very different mien is *Euonymus fortunei* 'Silver Queen', which doubles as an effective ground-cover shrub. Planted against a wall, it will eventually reach a height of some 10 ft (3 m). It has small oval leaves of fresh green and creamy white, taking on a pinkish tinge in winter which is

Euonymus fortunei 'Silver Queen', a small, compact shrub, grows taller against a wall

The evergreen *Clematis cirrhosa* var. *balearica* flowers from September to March

especially welcome. This is one of a range of cultivars of *E. fortunei* which have carved out a niche for themselves as highly decorative ground-cover shrubs. Others include 'Emerald Gaiety', in which the leaves are margined with silvery white and often flecked with pink in the winter months. It forms a mound some 2 ft tall and 2½ ft wide (60 by 76 cm). The very popular 'Emerald 'n' Gold', with rich golden yellow variegation and pink suffusions in winter is slightly smaller, while the even smaller 'Sunspot', which is rapidly coming to the fore, has dark green leaves enlivened by splashes of golden yellow. All grow well in any well drained soil of average quality, in sunshine or light shade.

The winter jasmine, *Jasminum nudiflorum*, is well known and very valuable for its bright yellow flowers in midwinter. The secret of keeping it in order is to prune it immediately after flowering has finished. If you don't, it can get in a real tangle. First you must form a framework of leading shoots, which are tied in to a trellis or some other support. Once that is established, then you annually, after flowering, reduce the laterals arising from these shoots to buds near the base. This brings order out of what can otherwise be chaos.

A winter-flowering climber for more favoured gardens is the fern-leaved clematis, *C. cirrhosa* var. *balearica*, which has prettily divided leaves, as the common name suggests, assuming a bronzy purple in winter. The creamy coloured bell flowers, spotted reddish purple within and less decorative than the foliage, are

175

With its neat habit of growth, *Hedera helix* 'Goldheart' is one of the finest variegated ivies

---

borne off and on throughout the winter. It can reach a height of 15 ft (4.5 m) or so and must be given a sheltered, sunny position.

And this brings me to the ivies, those indispensable climbers for year-round effect. Two of the most valuable must be the cultivars of *Hedera colchica*, 'Dentata Variegata' and 'Sulphur Heart' (or 'Paddy's Pride' as it used to be known). I have been amazed over the years just how much punishment both can take from the weather without any visible sign of distress. Once they get going, they can cover a vast expanse of wall space. 'Dentata Variegata' has very large, oval leaves which are an amalgam of palish green, grey green and creamy yellow; 'Sulphur Heart', with very slightly smaller, heart-shaped leaves, is a mixture of light and deeper green with bold areas of yellow. What would we do without them? In winter especially they are a real tonic.

Then, of course, there are the forms of the common ivy, *Hedera helix*. Some of the best for garden use are 'Goldheart', having dark green leaves with a central splash of bright yellow; 'Buttercup', bright yellow in full sun, with the green element increasing progressively if subjected to shade; and 'Ivalace', one of my favourites, with a very pretty five-lobed leaf of dark green.

The bright red stems of *Cornus alba* 'Sibirica' are even more striking against the foliage of *Elaeagnus* × *ebbingei* 'Gilt Edge'

—— Perennials of Consequence ——

Of the limited number of perennial plants which put on their display at this time of year, it is the hellebores which make by far the largest contribution. And what a contribution when one considers evergreen species and hybrids as diverse as the Corsican hellebore, *Helleborus corsicus*; the Christmas and Lenten roses, *H. niger* and *H. orientalis*; and the species which is so maligned by its name, *H. foetidus*, the so-called stinking hellebore, which only gives off an odour if its stems are crushed.

It always surprises me that the magnificent *Helleborus corsicus* does so well in this country, for it is, after all, a native of Corsica, Sardinia and the Balearic Islands, which have a very different climate. One of the best specimens I have ever seen was performing in Mull, western Scotland, admittedly in a snug, sheltered spot – as it needed to be on that windy island. It is indeed a sight to behold when in flower in March and April, the bold, tripartite leaves of greyish green surmounted by heads of pendant, bell-shaped, pale green flowers. Sometimes, too, it can be in flower in February. Like others of its kind, it prefers to grow in light shade in soil of good quality.

The Christmas rose, in flower from December to March, is a plant for a sheltered wall bed, although without the protection of a tall cloche, the attractive white blooms, with their prominent golden yellow stamens, are still likely to get badly damaged by weather and spoilt – a real consideration if they are wanted, as they so often are, for cutting for arrangement.

Helleborus orientalis is the group name for a number of hybrids which bear saucer-shaped flowers in a delightful range of colours from purplish plum to shades of maroon and pink and white with handsome petal markings of crimson or maroon. These plants, 1½ ft (45 cm) tall or perhaps a little more, provide a succession of blooms from February until early April and are especially useful for bringing to life shrub borders which are lack-lustre at that time of year.

It is usually March before the highly distinctive *Helleborus foetidus* comes into bloom with its pale green, suffused maroon flowers complemented handsomely by very dark green, almost black leaves, much divided into narrowly lanceolate segments. But flowering can start in February and it is an outstanding plant for shady positions.

Another plant of real importance is the beautiful Algerian *Iris*

Above: The wide-open flowers, spotted within, are typical of the Lenten roses
Below: *Helleborus corsicus* (left) does not bloom until its second year but is well worth waiting for; *Iris unguicularis* (right) seems to flower best in poor, dry soil where it is left undisturbed

A border in the famous winter garden at the University of Cambridge
Botanic Garden, with cornuses and *Helleborus foetidus*

unguicularis, of which there are quite a lot of forms in commerce, if only from single or very few sources in each case. Two of the best are the pale blue 'Walter Butt' and purple 'Mary Barnard', but it is usually early spring before they are in flower. The species itself flowers between October and March whenever the weather is reasonably mild, and really nothing could give more satisfaction than its lilac-mauve flowers, with their lovely yellow and white markings on the lower part of the petals, rising above the mass of grassy-looking foliage. The flower colouring can be variable, from the typical palish blue shades to purple. All are very attractive. The blooms last only a few days when cut, but even so are delightful in the home.

The pulmonarias or lungworts seem to have made a comeback in recent years, and very welcome that is too for they are excellent early-flowering perennials for shade. They also provide good ground cover with their large leaves and most are evergreen. In particular, I would draw attention to *Pulmonaria rubra* 'Redstart', which can be opening its rosy red flowers in early February, to continue in bloom until May or even June. The flowers have an admirable foil in the pale green leaves. *Pulmonaria saccharata* has dark green leaves heavily spotted with silver or grey, and a delightful form of it with pink and blue flowers is named 'Margery Fish'. These pulmonarias grow well in any soil which does not lack moisture.

The bergenias are among the best of perennials for ground cover, their mass of often very handsome, evergreen foliage providing effective weed barriers, quite apart from the spring display of showy blooms. Moreover, they flourish in any well drained soil of reasonable quality, in sunshine or light shade. Their interest in the present context is that some have foliage which colours up most attractively in winter. For instance, the leaves of 'Ballawley', one of the finest of the hybrids, turn a liver-red colour; 'Abenglut' becomes maroon with the reverse of the leaves plum-red; *B. cordifolia* 'Purpurea' is purplish; and *B. purpurascens* is reddish purple.

And don't forget the pretty little *Primula* 'Wanda', which often makes a brave show in late winter with its reddish purple flowers, in light shade or sunny positions.

Bulbs

Poise, perfection of form, classical beauty – one could heap the superlatives on snowdrops, those most welcome of all winter flowers. It is always a great moment when one goes out into the garden in mid-January or thereabouts and finds such forms of the common snowdrop, *Galanthus nivalis*, as 'Viridapicis' (with green tips to the outer segments of the flower as well as the inner ones) and the hybrid *G.* 'Atkinsii' in full bloom. Then, a little later, in February, the larger *G. elwesii* puts on its show. Of course, there are many other snowdrops, but these are what I would call in the mainstream of garden cultivation.

Snowdrops like shade and soil with a good moisture content. These easy plants can sometimes be quite tricky to establish from dry bulbs in autumn, but, increasingly, "green" plants are becoming available from bulb suppliers for planting in the spring.

Another bulbous plant which I would hate to be without in my garden is *Crocus tommasinianus*, a delightful little species which establishes itself readily in light shade or sunshine and soon carpets the ground in February with its lilac-mauve flowers. Forms like 'Whitewell Purple', reddish purple, and 'Ruby Giant', purple, are often in flower quite early in the month, and are less invasive than the species.

February-March flowering, too, are the *Crocus chrysanthus* forms such as the delectable white 'Snow Bunting'; 'E. A. Bowles', pale yellow with bronze basal markings; and 'Cream Beauty' and 'Blue Pearl', which have prominent orange-red and orange stigmata respectively to add greatly to their effectiveness. They are followed in flower in March by the Dutch hybrids, which make taller plants with larger flowers. Plant these in sunny positions near the front of a mixed border, around deciduous shrubs and indeed anywhere that they will prosper (they need shelter from cold winds) and give maximum visual enjoyment. Plant the corms 3 in. (7.5 cm) deep.

Wonderfully cheery, especially when it has the temerity to poke its buttercup-like, bright yellow flowers through snow in February, is the winter aconite, *Eranthis hyemalis*. The bright green leaves form a ruff around the flowers, and it naturalizes freely under trees or around shrubs. Plant the tubers 2 in. (5 cm) deep in late summer or early autumn, as soon as you can get hold of them, for like the snowdrops they don't like being out of the ground for long.

Above: *Galanthus* 'Atkinsii' is somewhat taller than the common snowdrop
Below: *Crocus chrysanthus* forms such as 'Cream Beauty' are among the earliest crocuses to flower

Above: *Eranthis hyemalis*, the winter aconite, may appear as early as January in mild weather
Below: *Iris histrioides* 'Major' has large weather-resistant flowers, lasting for several weeks

The precocious-flowering little forms of *Iris reticulata*, some 6 in. (15 cm) tall, have exquisitely moulded flowers in lovely shades of blue, violet and purple. They need a sunny, well-sheltered home where the soil is particularly well drained and preferably alkaline. They are ideal for planting in raised beds and troughs and, of course, for pockets in the rock garden. 'Cantab', a cultivar with soft blue colouring enhanced by orange markings on the falls (outer segments), is probably the best known. Slightly shorter and coming into flower rather earlier is the excellent Reticulata iris, *I. histrioides* 'Major'. It is also somewhat more robust, and a sight to savour with its dark blue flowers with white markings on the falls. Plant the bulbs 2 to 3 in. (5–7 cm) deep in September or as soon as possible in autumn.

A hardy cyclamen which comes within our purview is the charming little *Cyclamen coum*, a mere 3 in. (7.5 cm) tall and with miniature blooms typical of the genus borne above rounded, dark green leaves, which may have silver markings. The flower colour is variable – anything from shades of red to pink and white – and it blooms between the turn of the year and late February. It is best given a lightly shaded position, humus-rich soil and especially good drainage. Plant the tubers about 1 in. (2.5 cm) deep in early autumn, but better still, if you can, find a nursery which offers pot-grown specimens for sale. Start with these for preference, for tubers offered dry can be difficult to establish if out of the ground for some time.

The pretty pale blue squill, *Scilla tubergeniana*, with stylish darker blue banding down each segment of the flower, leads its clan into bloom by a margin of some weeks. It opens its flowers in February and early March, and is followed by the fine deep blue form of the Siberian squill, *S. sibirica*, known as 'Spring Beauty', which with a height of about 8 in. (20 cm) is twice the size of *tubergeniana*. Both kinds increase freely. The bulbs should be planted 3 in. (7.5 cm) deep in autumn and be left alone to increase until they have become overcrowded, when they can be lifted, divided and replanted in late summer.

There are forms of the handsome *Anemone blanda* which come into flower in February and March – for instance, 'White Splendour', the pink 'Charmer' and 'Violet Star'. All are about 4 in. (10 cm) tall. They associate very well with deciduous shrubs, which in the summer can provide some shade from the sun. Plant the tubers 2 in. (5 cm) deep in early autumn.

What else? Well, certainly the spring snowflake, *Leucojum vernum*, the bulbous plant which looks like an oversized snowdrop. And very fine it is, with its bold, strap-shaped leaves of dark green complementing perfectly the shapely white flowers with

their green markings on the tips of the segments. I like even better the east European variety of this European native – *carpathicum*, in which the segment markings are yellow rather than green. In mild winters, both are in flower by late February or early March (even early January in 1989), so fitting comfortably into this winter survey.

One can include also some of the earliest of the *Narcissus cyclamineus* hybrids, those spendidly garden-worthy derivatives of this species crossed with trumpet daffodils. The exquisite *N. cyclamineus* itself bears its bright yellow, cyclamen-like flowers in February and March, but needs a moist soil to succeed. What beauty there is in the long trumpet and swept-back segments of its flowers. Of the hybrids, 'February Gold', as the name implies, is very early coming into bloom, although it is more likely to be the beginning of March than February. 'Peeping Tom', some 14 to 15 in. (35–38 cm) tall as opposed to the 12 in. (30 cm) of 'February Gold', also flowers in early March. Another lovely early form is the deep yellow 'Tête-à-Tête', a mere 6 in. (15 cm) tall and carrying several blooms on each stem. Everything depends on the weather and the severity of the winter as to just when these and other Cyclamineus hybrids start their display. They are marvellous for growing below deciduous shrubs, and can transform areas which would otherwise be just a mess of bare stems at that time. Plant the bulbs 3 to 4 in. (7.5–10 cm) deep in September or as soon as possible thereafter.

(For some further suggestions, see the Wisley Handbook, *Growing Dwarf Bulbs*.)

POSTSCRIPT

Hopefully, there is enough in this to whet the appetite and indicate some of the pleasures which the winter garden is capable of providing. One of the most agreeable aspects of the British climate is its clearly defined seasonal differences – differences which provide our gardens with major sources of interest. Winter, no less than spring, summer and autumn, has much to offer.

The variable *Cyclamen coum* usually begins flowering in January

Index

Page numbers in **bold** type
refer to illustrations